BONUS:
30 DAY MEAL PLAN

SIMPLE & QUICK
MEDITERRANEAN
DIET COOKBOOK
FOR BEGINNERS

150

**NUTRITIOUS & EASY RECIPES TO
MAKE IN 30 MINUTES OR LESS
TO INCREASE LONGEVITY, WELL-BEING,
AND DEVELOP A VITAL LIFESTYLE.**

LEONORA GROVER

YOUR JOURNEY TO A HEALTHIER, HAPPIER YOU BEGINS NOW!

CHECK OUT PAGE 96 FOR BONUS VIDEO RECIPES.

TABLE OF CONTENTS

TABLE OF CONTENT

LIVE SIMPLY, EAT WELL, AND AGE GRACEFULLY. THAT'S THE MEDITERRANEAN WAY.

- GRANDMA JOE

INTRODUCTION

Did you know that people living in countries bordering the Mediterranean Sea consistently rank among the healthiest and happiest in the world? It's not just sunshine and scenic views – it's the food! The Mediterranean diet, a celebration of fresh, flavorful ingredients, and a relaxed approach to eating is your key to unlocking a healthier, happier you.

Forget fad diets and restrictive meal plans. Forget counting calories, that's for boring people. The Mediterranean diet is all about fresh, sun-kissed ingredients that'll make your body do a jig. Think plump tomatoes like little flavor bombs, glistening olives that'll have you licking your fingers, and fish so fresh it practically leaps off the plate. Drenched in the good stuff – that's right, extra virgin olive oil – every bite's gonna be an explosion of taste that'll leave you wanting more.

This book is your one-stop shop for making the Mediterranean diet a delicious reality in your busy life. This cookbook combines these elements to create a collection of 150 simple and quick recipes that are bursting with taste and nourishment. Forget spending hours in the kitchen! Each recipe is designed to be prepared in 30 minutes or less, making it perfect for busy weeknights or lazy weekend mornings. Let's savor the moment, not the dishes! We can enjoy both the meal and the company by keeping things simple while prepping and cleaning.

I'll guide you through creating vegetarian delights, seafood sensations, and poultry perfection, all inspired by the diverse culinary traditions of the Mediterranean. Enjoy dishes that are not only unbelievable tasty, but also can be a superhero against the heart woes, strokes, wonky blood sugar (type 2 diabetes), and even some nasty cancers. Research suggests that including olive oil in your diet can improve cholesterol, regulate blood sugar, and reduce inflammation – all are contributing to a healthier you and a stronger defense against chronic conditions. Now get cooking!

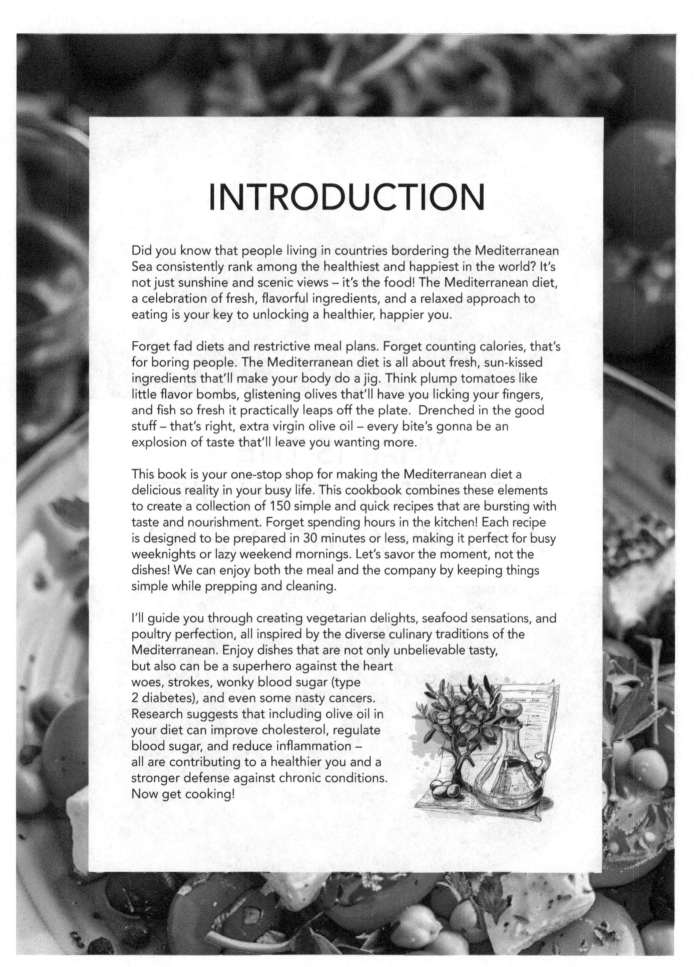

WHAT IS THE MEDITERRANEAN DIET AND WHY CHOOSE IT?

Listen up, you gorgeous lot! There's a secret simmering in the sunshine, a way of life that's got folks kicking around like teenagers well past their hundredth birthday. I'm talkin' about the **Blue Zones**, these pockets of paradise where people defy the clock with their zest for life and longevity.

These folks, especially the twinkle-eyed citizens of Ikaria, a little Greek village where centenarians are as common as figs on a summer's day, have sorted the whole living-to-a-hundred thing. Here's the juicy secret: it ain't about deprivation. It's about dialing up life's delicious dials.

Imagine this: sun-kissed vegetables bursting with flavor, fat, juicy olives swimming in sunshine-gold olive oil, and fish so fresh it practically flips you the fin on its way to the pan. Vibrant salads that look like edible rainbows, slow-cooked stews that simmer with love and laughter, and glasses of deep red wine shared with the ones who make your heart sing beneath a canopy of stars.

Now, you might be thinking, "Hey, lady, I live in a concrete jungle where kale is considered a delicacy and sun-shine comes with a side of traffic fumes." Don't you fret your bonny head about that? The beauty of the Mediter-ranean way of life is that it's about simplicity, not sacrifice. It's about ditching the processed grub and stress-filled days for authentic, delicious food that nourishes your body and soul. Think of long walks by the beach with the sand between your toes instead of pounding a treadmill at a germ-infested gym. Surround yourself with the people who make you laugh until your sides ache, who fill your life with sunshine even on the grayest days.

This ain't some limp lettuce and steamed fish kind of life, my dears. This is about making every meal a fiesta for your senses, every day an adventure that sparks joy, and every sip of wine a celebration of life itself.

So ditch the diet dust and embrace the Mediterranean magic. It might not be a magic potion, but trust me, your taste buds, ticker, Gut, heart, skin, hair, and of course, soul will thank you for it. You might find yourself living as long and luscious as a summer spent island-hopping in Greece!

MEDITERRANEAN DIET PYRAMID

The Mediterranean Food Pyramid is a helpful tool for understanding the core principles of this healthy eating pattern. It emphasizes fresh, plant-based foods, healthy fats, and moderate portions of protein sources. By following this visual guide, you can adopt a delicious and nutritious way of eating that can benefit your overall well-being.

SWEATS & RED MEATS
Enjoy monthly or small amounts

EGGS, POULTRY, ETC.
Enjoy 1-2x/weekly

SEAFOOD, FISH, OMEGA-3 RICH FOODS
Enjoy >3x/weekly

WHOLE GRAINS, LEGUMES, FRUIT, VEGETABLES, HEALTHY FATS, HERBS & SPICES
Enjoy daily

DAILY PHYSICAL ACTIVITY, MEAL & FAMILY/FRIENDS TIME

BENEFITS OF THE MEDITERRANEAN DIET: UNLOCKING LONGEVITY, WELL-BEING & VITAL LIFESTYLE

Longevity and disease prevention:

Reduced risk of chronic disease: Documented proof shows the Mediterranean diet can be a superhero against heart woes, strokes, wonky blood sugar (type 2 diabetes), and even some nasty cancers. It's all about chewing on natural, wholesome foods, drenching everything in delicious olive oil (the good fat!), and keeping protein portions in check. This boss diet keeps your whole body humming along smoothly. Studies even show it sweetens your cholesterol levels, chills out your blood sugar, and calms inflammation - all adding up to a shield against those chronic creeps.

Brainpower: The Mediterranean diet - think lots of veggies, fish, and olive oil - is like brain food! It can help you think faster, remember more, and even keep your mind sharp as you age. Plus, it might help you avoid getting dementia down the road.

Eating for healthy blood sugar: Filling your plate with whole grains, beans, and fruits helps keep your blood sugar in check, which is great for both preventing and managing diabetes.

Cancer Prevention: Eating a diet packed with antioxidants and anti-inflammatory stuff might help lower your chances of getting some cancers.

Feeling good and balanced made easy

Mood and Mental Health: Ditch the frown! The Mediterranean diet can help you feel less bummed and anxious. It's all about eating a good mix of yummy foods, hanging out with loved ones, and chilling out more. This all adds up to feeling fantastic overall.

Weight Management: Say goodbye to hanger! Sticking to whole, unprocessed foods keeps you feeling fuller for longer, so you're less likely to stuff yourself. Plus, the healthy fats help your body regulate hormones that control how hungry you feel.

Energy Levels: No more afternoon slumps! The Mediterranean diet gives you a steady stream of energy throughout the day because it has a good balance of carbs, protein, and healthy fats. This keeps you feeling energized and focused.

HOW TO GET STARTED WITH THE MEDITERRANEAN DIET

The Mediterranean diet isn't just about food; it's a way of life inspired by the sunshine-soaked cultures bordering the Mediterranean Sea. This dietary pattern emphasizes fresh, flavorful ingredients and focuses on enjoying meals with loved ones. Ready to dive in? Here's how to get started:

Grocery Shopping for the Mediterranean Masterpiece:
Put down the phones and sharpen your knives! We're about to craft a dish that'll tantalize your taste buds and turn heads (metaphorically, of course, this is a professional kitchen). Think of your pantry and fridge as a pristine artist's palette, primed for a vibrant explosion of Mediterranean flavours. Let's get prepped with this essential shopping list:

Liquid Gold: Why You Should Treasure Olive Oil

Olive oil ain't your granny's salad dressing, it's the nectar of the gods! Drizzled down from the Mediterranean sun for centuries, this liquid gold ain't just for cookin'. It's a full-on flavour fiesta.

Health Benefits: Healthy fats that keep your heart happy, antioxidants that fight off nasties, and vitamins that make you glow from the inside out. Boom! Now that's sexy, yeah?

Culinary Versatility: From searing a perfect steak to drizzling over a fresh salad, olive oil enhances many dishes. Its various grades cater to high-heat cooking or delicate finishing touches.

Rich Flavor Profile: High-quality olive oil boasts a symphony of flavors, ranging from grassy and peppery to buttery and fruity.

The Home of Your Next Olive Oil:
While Tunisia, Portugal, and France are all respectable olive oil producers, Greece, Italy, and Spain are definitely the champions, boasting time-honored techniques and distinct flavor profiles:
Greece: Greek olive oil is known for its grassy, slightly bitter notes, often attributed to the Koroneiki olive variety. Crete, in particular, is renowned for producing some of the world's finest EVOO (Extra Virgin Olive Oil). And that's definitely my favorite region!
Italy: Italian olive oil tends to be bolder, with peppery and fruity characteristics. Tuscany and Sicily are regions particularly celebrated for their olive oil.
Spain: Spanish olive oil shines with its fruity and nutty notes.

Choosing Your Perfect Olive Oil:
The best choice ultimately depends on your taste preference. Do you crave a robust oil for dipping bread? Perhaps a grassy oil to complement a fish dish? Explore both Greek and Italian EVOOs to discover your favorites.

Remember: Look for labels that mention "Extra Virgin Olive Oil" and a protected designation of origin (PDO) for the highest quality and authenticity.

A DRIZZLE OF OLIVE OIL A DAY KEEPS THE DOCTOR AWAY

Fruits and Veggies: Feast for Your Eyes (and Gut): Pile your cart high with a dazzling rainbow of fruits and veggies! Think like Mother Nature's artist and go for what's in season and local whenever you can. Juicy tomatoes, cool cucumbers, vibrant peppers, leafy greens like kale or spinach, plump berries, and refreshing melons - the only limit is your imagination!

Whole Grains: The Powerhouse for Your Plate: Stock your pantry with whole-grain champions like brown rice, quinoa, and whole-wheat bread and pasta. These slow-burning superstars will keep you energized and deliver a hefty dose of nutrients your body craves.

Legumes: Tiny Titans of Nutrition: Beans, lentils, and chickpeas are protein and fiber powerhouses in disguise! Don't be afraid to experiment - there are tons of varieties to explore, each adding a unique twist and texture to your meals.

Fish and Seafood: Dive into Deliciousness: Aim to make fish and shellfish your fin-tastic friends 2-3 times a week. Fatty fish like salmon and sardines are overflowing with omega-3s, which are great for your heart.

Nuts and Seeds: Nature's Mighty Munchies: A small handful of nuts and seeds each day is a sprinkle of healthy fats, protein, and fiber. Almonds, walnuts, flaxseeds, and pumpkin seeds are all nutritional all-stars.

Herbs and Spices: The Secret Weapon of Flavor: Fresh herbs are the secret weapon of the Mediterranean diet. They add magic to any dish! Here's a cheat sheet to get you started:

Basil: The fragrant king of pesto, perfect for summer salads and tomato dishes.

Oregano: A Greek and Italian essential, it adds depth to pizzas, pastas, and roasted veggies.

Parsley: This versatile herb brings a touch of freshness to salads, sauces, and dips.

Rosemary: With its piney kick, rosemary is a perfect match for lamb, roasted potatoes, and focaccia bread.

Thyme: This culinary chameleon complements everything from chicken and fish to roasted vegetables and soups.

Garlic: The Humble Powerhouse. Though unassuming in appearance, garlic lends its depth and pungency to an astounding array of dishes. From creamy pasta sauces to fiery stir-fries, meats, and roasted vegetables, garlic's versatility knows no bounds.

Mint: A refreshing breath of fresh air for salads, dips like tzatziki, and even summer cocktails.

Coriander/Cilantro: These fragrant leaves offer a citrusy, nutty punch. Toasted or ground, they can elevate curries, spice rubs, and even add a unique twist to roasted vegetables.

Here's how to dive headfirst into the delicious world of the Mediterranean diet:

Plan Your Meals: Spend some time each week planning what you'll cook. This recipe book is your treasure map to deliciousness!

Shop Like a Farmer: Take advantage of fresh, seasonal produce at your local farmer's market or grocery store. Think summer berries and plump winter squash!

Become a Kitchen Captain: Cooking at home gives you the power to control exactly what goes into your food and how much you eat. You're the boss!

Read Food Labels: Be a food label detective! Watch out for hidden sugars, sodium, and unhealthy fats lurking in packaged goods.

Make Small Swaps: Instead of butter, whip out the olive oil for a heart-healthy twist. Whole grains are rockstars, so ditch refined options. Make fish or chicken your main squeeze most of the week, and red meat can be a special occasion guest.

Treat Yourself, Tiger: Don't become a hangry monster! Enjoy treats in moderation – the Mediterranean diet is all about finding a happy balance and savoring the good stuff.

Chill Out, Chef: Cooking and eating should be fun, not stressful. Don't worry about making everything picture-perfect.

LIVING THE MEDITERRANEAN LIFESTYLE

Chill Island Vibes: Move Your Body, Find Your Zen, and Crew Up

Alright, listen up! Forget six-pack abs and weird protein shakes – we're talking about living, not existing! The Mediterraneans know what's good. Sun-kissed skin? Check. Delicious food that makes your taste buds do the samba? Double-check. But it's more than that, yeah? It's about feeling alive like you've got the whole damn ocean pulsing through your veins.

Move Like There's No Tomorrow (But at a Chill Pace)

First things first, gotta get your body moving. Not just for lookin' good on the beach (although that's a definite perk), but for feeling like a total stunner from the inside out. Think about your body like a finely tuned engine. Exercise gets that heart pumpin', blood flowin', and keeps your immune system fightin' fit. But that's not all! We're talkin' serious mood elevation, babes. Forget that sluggish feeling after a greasy fry-up or a night of social media scrolling. Exercise gives you a hit of dopamine, the real deal, not that cheap kind. This is the good stuff that builds your confidence and makes you wanna shout "hell yeah!" from the rooftops. So, ditch the elevator and take the stairs; feel those legs burnin' - that's your body saying "thank you!".

Find an activity that gets you groovin', like dancing to music that makes you wanna move every inch. A walk along the beach with the sand between your toes, gardening, a bike ride that winds through those sexy olive groves – that's the kind of exercise we're talking about. Join a team, meet new people, and sweat it out together – that's a recipe for feeling good. Gear up for some right cheeky leg action. I'm talkin' ten thousand steps a day, yeah? That's right, ten thousand! Trust me, by the end of it, you'll be feelin' like a minted fit bird. Legs toned, booty peachy, you won't regret it, not a bit. The docs say that if you exercise for one hour, you can add three extra hours to your lifespan! Remember, exercise ain't a punishment; it's a celebration of your amazing body. Get movin', feel the endorphins rushin', and watch your confidence take flight.

Find Your Calm in the Crazy

Now, life can be a right old caper, but you gotta slow down sometimes. The Mediterraneans get this. That afternoon siesta? Not for the wimps! It's a chance to recharge your batteries, like taking a power nap for your whole soul. Wake up feeling refreshed, ready to tackle the rest of the day with a twinkle in your eye. And hey, if a siesta isn't your vibe, find what chills you out. Meditation? Yoga that makes your body pretzel like a pro? Do what makes you feel zen. And let's calm down a little bit. Like the Greeks say, "siga, siga", means „slow, slow" – gotta take it nice and easy.

Crew Love: You're Not in This Alone

Here's the real secret sauce, though: the people. Food in the Mediterranean? Not a solo act. It's a feast shared with mates and family, laughter bouncing off the walls like sunshine. Strong bonds, deep connections – that's what keeps the soul happy. Feeling like you belong, like you're part of something bigger? That's powerful stuff. It chases away the blues faster than you can say "ouzo." The Mediterranean lifestyle isn't about being perfect, it's about finding your rhythm. Move your body, find your calm and connect with the people who make you smile. That's the recipe for a life sizzling with happiness, yeah? Now, go out there and live a little!

BREAKFAST

Sun-Kissed Scramble Wrap

COOK: 20 MINS I SERVES: 1 I CAL: 260 KCAL

Ingredients

- 1/4 cup chopped cherry tomatoes
- 1/4 cup crumbled feta cheese
- 1/4 cup baby spinach, chopped
- Salt and pepper to taste
- 1 whole wheat tortilla
- 2 large eggs
- 1 tbsp olive oil

Instructions:

1. Scramble eggs in a pan with olive oil until cooked through. Season with salt and pepper.
2. Add chopped cherry tomatoes and spinach to the pan. Cook for 2-3 minutes until tomatoes soften and spinach wilts slightly.
3. Remove from heat and stir in feta cheese.
4. Warm the tortilla in a dry pan or microwave for a few seconds.
5. Spread the egg mixture onto the center of the tortilla.
6. Fold the bottom of the tortilla up, then fold in the sides. Roll up tightly and serve immediately.

Smoked Salmon & Avocado Wrap

COOK: 10 MINS I SERVES: 1 I CAL: 380 KCAL

Ingredients

- 2 slices smoked salmon
- 1/4 cup mashed avocado
- 1 tbsp crumbled goat cheese or feta cheese
- 1 small handful of baby arugula
- Salt and lemon pepper to taste
- 1 whole wheat tortilla

Instructions:

1. Spread mashed avocado onto the center of the tortilla.
2. Layer smoked salmon on top of the avocado.
3. Sprinkle with crumbled goat cheese / feta cheese and baby arugula.
4. Season with salt and lemon pepper to taste.
5. Fold the bottom of the tortilla up, then fold in the sides. Roll up tightly and serve immediately. This ain't yo' mama's wrap, this is pure, unadulterated deliciousness!

Mediterranean Tuna Melt Wrap

COOK: 15 MINS I SERVES: 1 I CAL: 340 KCAL

Ingredients

- 1 (5 oz) can tuna in water, flaked
- 1 tablespoon olive oil
- 1 tablespoon lemon juice
- 1/4 cup chopped red onion
- Pinch of dried oregano
- 1/4 cup chopped kalamata olives (or any available black olives you have)
- 1/4 cup crumbled feta cheese
- 1/4 cup chopped fresh parsley
- Salt and black pepper to taste
- 1 large whole wheat tortilla
- 1 roma tomato, sliced (optional)
- Handful of baby spinach (optional)

Instructions:

1. Combine flaked tuna, olive oil, lemon juice, red onion, kalamata olives, feta cheese, parsley, oregano, salt, and pepper in a medium bowl. Mix well.
2. Heat a large skillet over medium heat (optional). If you prefer a toasted wrap, place the tortilla in the dry skillet and cook for about 30 seconds per side, until lightly browned and warmed through.
3. Spread the tuna mixture evenly over the warmed tortilla (or unwarmed, if you prefer).
4. Add sliced tomato and baby spinach (if using) and fold the bottom of the tortilla up and over the filling.
5. A tight wrap is a happy wrap. Slice that bad boy in half and there you have it – a taste bud explosion ready to devour!

Creamy Ricotta Toast, Honey & Berries

COOK: 10 MINS I SERVES: 2 I CAL: 430 KCAL

Ingredients

- 2 slices whole wheat toast
- 1/4 cup ricotta cheese
- 1 tbsp honey
- 1/4 cup fresh berries (blueberries, raspberries, cherries or strawberries). Or any other fruits (for example, pears or peaches)
- Pinch of ground cinnamon (optional)

Instructions:

1. Toast whole wheat bread slices.
2. Spread ricotta cheese evenly on the toast.
3. Drizzle with honey and top with fresh berries.
4. A sprinkle of cinnamon, if you're feeling a bit extra, like a warm hug on a chilly morning. This is breakfast that'll leave you wanting more.

Sun-Dried Tomato, Goat Cheese Toast, Arugula

COOK: 10 MINS I SERVES: 1 I CAL: 280 KCAL

Ingredients

- 1/4 cup chopped sun-dried tomatoes (not packed in oil)
- 1 slice whole-wheat bread
- 1 tbsp goat cheese
- 1/4 cup baby arugula
- 1 tbsp olive oil
- Pinch of red pepper flakes (optional)
- Salt and freshly ground black pepper to taste

Instructions:

1. Toast the whole-wheat bread slice in a toaster until golden brown.
2. While the bread toasts, spread the goat cheese evenly over the toasted bread.
3. Top with chopped sun-dried tomatoes.
4. Add a generous handful of baby arugula to the toast.
5. (Optional) Sprinkle a pinch of dried oregano over the arugula.
6. Last but not least, a drizzle of the good stuff – extra virgin olive oil.
7. Season with salt and freshly ground black pepper to taste (optional) for a touch of heat. Grab a plate!

Scrambled Eggs with Feta & Tomatoes Toast

COOK: 15 MINS I SERVES: 1 I CAL: 420 KCAL

Ingredients

- 2 large eggs
- 1 tbsp olive oil
- 1/4 cup chopped tomatoes
- 1/4 cup crumbled feta cheese
- 1 slice whole-wheat or full grain bread, toasted
- Pinch of dried oregano
- Salt and pepper to taste

Instructions:

1. Crack the eggs into a bowl and whisk them well with a pinch of salt and pepper.
2. Heat the olive oil in a non-stick pan over medium heat.
3. Pour the whisked eggs into the pan and let them cook undisturbed for a minute or two until the bottom begins to set.
4. Gently push the cooked egg from the edges towards the center of the pan with a spatula, allowing the uncooked egg to flow underneath. Continue this process until the eggs are almost cooked through.
5. Add the chopped tomatoes to the pan and cook for another minute or until softened slightly.
6. Sprinkle the crumbled feta cheese and dried oregano over the scrambled eggs.
7. Fold everything together and let the cheese melt for a few seconds.
8. Meanwhile, toast a slice of bread.
9. Transfer the scrambled eggs to the toasted bread.
10. Season with additional salt and pepper to taste (optional).

Whipped Feta & Roasted Vegetables Toast

COOK: 20 MINS I SERVES: 1 I CAL: 310 KCAL

Ingredients

- 1 slice whole wheat bread or full grain, toasted
- 1/4 cup crumbled feta cheese
- 1/4 cup roasted vegetables (zucchini, peppers, eggplant), chopped
- 1 tbsp chopped fresh mint (optional)
- 1/2 tbsp olive oil
- Pinch of dried oregano, pinch of dried thyme
- Salt and freshly ground black pepper to taste

Instructions:

1. In a small bowl, mash the feta cheese with a fork until slightly creamy.
2. Preheat your oven to 400°F (200°C). Toss chopped vegetables with olive oil, thyme, oregano, salt, and pepper. Spread on a baking sheet in a single layer and roast for 10-15 minutes or until tender and slightly browned. While the vegetables roast, toast your bread slice in a toaster or pan until golden brown. Spread the whipped feta cheese on the toasted bread.
3. Top the toasted bread with the roasted vegetables and mint (if using). Enjoy immediately!

Lemony Shrimp Scampi Toast

COOK: 15 MINS I SERVES: 2 I CAL: 380 KCAL

Ingredients

- 2 slices whole-wheat bread
- 4-5 cooked and deveined shrimp
- 1 tbsp olive oil
- 1 tbsp chopped garlic
- 1/4 cup chopped cherry tomatoes
- 1 tbsp lemon juice
- 1 tbsp chopped fresh parsley
- 1/4 cup dry white wine (or chicken broth)
- Salt and pepper

Instructions:

1. Toast the whole-wheat bread slices in a toaster until golden brown.
2. While the bread toasts, heat olive oil in a pan over medium heat.
3. Add the shrimp and cook for 2-3 minutes per side, or until opaque and pink throughout. Remove shrimp from the pan and set aside.
4. Use the same pan, add the chopped garlic and cook for 30 seconds until fragrant.
5. Add the cherry tomatoes and cook for another minute, allowing them to soften slightly.
6. Pour in the white wine (or broth) and lemon juice, scraping any browned bits from the bottom of the pan.
7. Bring the sauce to a simmer and cook for 2-3 minutes, allowing it to reduce slightly.
8. Taste the sause, season with salt and pepper.
9. Add the cooked shrimp back to the pan and toss with the sauce for another minute to heat through.
10. Spoon the shrimp scampi mixture over the toasted bread slices.
11. Garnish with fresh chopped parsley for a pop of color and freshness.

Poached Egg & Salmon Toast with Avocado

COOK: 15 MINS I SERVES: 1 I CAL: 410 KCAL

Ingredients

- 1 slice whole-wheat or full-grain bread, toasted
- 1/2 ripe avocado, mashed
- 3 oz smoked salmon, flaked
- 1 large egg
- Pinch of dried oregano
- 1 tbsp white wine vinegar (or apple cider vinegar)
- Salt and freshly ground black pepper to taste
- Extra virgin olive oil (for drizzling)
- Lemon wedge (optional)

Instructions:

1. Toast the whole-wheat or full-grain bread slice in a toaster until golden brown.
2. While the bread toasts, prepare the poached egg. Grab a small saucepan and add enough water to reach about 2 inches. Heat it on low until simmering. Add the white wine vinegar.
3. Crack an egg on the counter, letting it spill softly into a waiting bowl. Swirl a spoon in simmering water, creating a gentle whirlpool. Carefully swirl the water and then gently slip the egg into the center.
4. Cook the egg for 3-4 minutes until the whites are set but the yolk is still runny.
5. Meanwhile, spread the mashed avocado on the toasted bread. Top with the flaked smoked salmon.
6. With a gentle touch, use the slotted spoon to scoop the poached egg from the simmering water. Carefully maneuver it over the salmon fillet and release it for a delicious combination.
7. Season with a pinch of dried oregano, salt, and freshly ground black pepper. Drizzle with a touch of extra virgin olive oil (optional). Serve immediately with a lemon wedge for squeezing over the dish (optional).

Spicy Black Bean & Avocado Toast, Lime Crema

COOK: 15 MINS I SERVES: 1 I CAL: 410 KCAL

Ingredients

- 1 slice whole-wheat or full grain bread, toasted
- 1/2 avocado, mashed
- 1/3 cup canned black beans, drained and rinsed
- 1/4 cup chopped tomato
- 1 tbsp chopped red onion
- 1/4 cup plain Greek yogurt
- 1 tbsp chopped fresh cilantro (plus extra for garnish)
- 1 tsp lime juice
- 1/4 tsp ground cumin
- Pinch of chili powder (optional)
- Salt and pepper to taste

Instructions:

1. In a small bowl, combine Greek yogurt, chopped cilantro, lime juice, cumin, chili powder (if using), and a pinch of salt and pepper. Stir to create a creamy sauce.
2. Toast your bread and spread it with mashed avocado.
3. Top with black beans, chopped tomato, and red onion. Drizzle with the cilantro lime crema and, finally, a little green garnish – fresh cilantro, to make it pretty (but we all know the real star of the show is underneath).

Chickpea Scramble Toast with Feta & Herbs

COOK: 10 MINS I SERVES: 1 I CAL: 290 KCAL

Ingredients

- 1/4 cup cooked chickpeas, rinsed and mashed with a fork
- 1 tbsp chopped red onion
- 1/4 tsp turmeric powder
- Pinch of black pepper
- 1/2 tbsp olive oil
- 1 tbsp chopped fresh herbs (parsley)
- 1 slice whole-wheat toast
- 1 tbsp crumbled feta cheese
- 1 large egg

Instructions:

1. Mash chickpeas.
2. Sauté onion in olive oil, add spices and cook for 1 minute.
3. Scramble egg, then combine with chickpeas and onion mixture.
4. Toast bread.
5. Assemble: toast, scramble, feta. Don't forget the herbs, fresh and fragrant, like a kiss on the cheek. Add hot sauce for spice if you like. There you have it, my lovelies – a breakfast that's as good lookin' as it is tasty.

Sweet Potato & Goat Cheese Omelette

COOK: 15 MINS I SERVES: 1 I CAL: 340 KCAL

Ingredients

- 2 large eggs
- 1/2 cup cooked and mashed sweet potato
- 1/4 cup crumbled goat cheese
- 1 tbsp chopped fresh mint
- 1/4 tsp ground cinnamon
- Pinch of ground ginger
- 1 tbsp olive oil
- Salt and pepper to taste

Instructions:

1. In a bowl, combine your eggs with a sprinkle of salt and pepper. Use a whisk to create a smooth, well-blended mixture.
2. Stir in mashed sweet potato, goat cheese, mint, cinnamon, and ginger.
3. Heat olive oil in a skillet over medium heat. Then, carefully pour in the egg mixture, tilting the pan to evenly distribute the eggs across the bottom. Lift and fold: gently push cooked egg towards the center with your spatula, letting the runny part flow underneath.
4. Cook for 3-4 minutes, or until the bottom is golden brown and the center is almost set. Enjoy!

Tropical Oats with Mango & Chia Seeds

COOK: 10 MINS | SERVES: 1 | CAL: 270 KCAL

Ingredients

- 1/4 cup chopped fresh mango
- 1/4 cup chopped pineapple
- 1/4 cup chia seeds
- 1/4 cup coconut milk (unsweetened)
- 1/4 cup water
- 1/4 tsp vanilla extract

Instructions:

1. Combine rolled oats, chia seeds, coconut milk, water, and vanilla extract in a mason jar or container. Stir well.
2. Fold in chopped mango and pineapple.
3. Refrigerate overnight.
4. In the morning, enjoy as is or top with additional chopped fresh fruit (or berries) for a tropical flavor boost. This ain't your boring old porridge; this is tropical, this is delicious, and this is breakfast that'll leave you wanting more!

Almond & Orange Blossom Chia Pudding

COOK: 10 MINS | SERVES: 1 | CAL: 380 KCAL

Ingredients

- 1/3 cup chia seeds
- 1 cup unsweetened almond milk
- 1 tbsp honey (or maple syrup)
- 1/2 tsp orange blossom water
- 1/4 cup sliced almonds
- 1/4 cup fresh berries and orange fillets (optional)

Instructions:

1. In a bowl or jar, combine almond milk, honey, the chia seeds and orange blossom water. Whisk well to ensure everything is evenly distributed. Seal the container tightly and refrigerate for at least 4 hours, preferably overnight to allow the chia seeds to absorb the liquid and thicken.
2. When ready to serve, stir the pudding well.
3. Top with sliced almonds, oranges and fresh berries (optional).

Creamy Fig & Walnut Overnight Oats

COOK: 10 MINS I SERVES: 1 I CAL: 410 KCAL

Ingredients

- 1/2 cup rolled oats
- 1/4 cup chopped dried figs, 1 or 2 fresh figs to decorate
- 1/4 cup chopped walnuts
- 1/2 cup milk (dairy or non-dairy)
- 1/4 cup plain Greek yogurt
- 1 tbsp honey
- 1/4 tsp ground cinnamon
- Pinch of sea salt

Instructions:

1. Combine rolled oats, dried figs, chopped walnuts, milk, Greek yogurt, honey, cinnamon, and salt in a mason jar or container. Stir well. Tip: You can always try new combinations such as apple, honey, cinnamon walnuts, or just add bananas for a creamy touch..
2. Refrigerate overnight.
3. In the morning, enjoy chilled or briefly warmed in the microwave for a warm breakfast. This is breakfast that whispers sweet nothings and leaves you satisfied. Now, get to it!

Greek Yogurt Power Bowl with Berries & Granola

COOK: 10 MINS I SERVES: 1 I CAL: 460 KCAL

Ingredients

- 1/2 cup plain Greek yogurt
- 1/4 cup granola (choose a low-sugar variety for a healthier option)
- 1/3 cup mixed berries (fresh or frozen)
- 1/4 cup chopped walnuts
- 1 tbsp honey
- 1/4 tsp ground cinnamon

Instructions:

1. In a bowl, layer Greek yogurt, granola, berries, and walnuts.
2. Drizzle with honey and sprinkle with cinnamon. There you have it, a breakfast that's good enough to eat with your eyes closed (but don't, gotta see this beauty!). Dig in and enjoy!

Strawberry Balsamic Oats

COOK: 10 MINS | SERVES: 1 | CAL: 330 KCAL

Ingredients

- 1/2 cup rolled oats
- 1/2 cup unsweetened almond milk
- 1/4 cup chopped fresh strawberries
- 1 tbsp chopped walnuts, toasted
- 1 tsp balsamic vinegar
- Pinch of ground cinnamon
- Pinch of sea salt
- 1 tsp honey

Instructions:

1. In a jar or container with a lid, combine rolled oats, almond milk, balsamic vinegar, honey, cinnamon, and sea salt. Stir well.
2. Gently fold in chopped strawberries.
3. Secure the lid and refrigerate overnight (at least 8 hours).
4. Top with toasted walnuts in the morning for a satisfying crunch. Come morning, you'll be greeted by a breakfast ready to rock your world.

Spicy Pumpkin Spice Oats

COOK: 10 MINS | SERVES: 1 | CAL: 375 KCAL

Ingredients

- 1/2 cup rolled oats
- 1/2 cup canned pumpkin puree (unsweetened)
- 1/2 cup plant-based milk (almond, soy, oat)
- 1 tbsp chopped walnuts, toasted
- 1/4 tsp ground cinnamon
- 1/2 tsp pumpkin spice blend
- Pinch of ground ginger
- Honey to sweet
- Pomegranate or apple slices for decoration

Instructions:

1. In a jar or container with a lid, combine rolled oats, pumpkin puree, plant-based milk, pumpkin spice blend, cinnamon, and ginger. Stir well.
2. Secure the lid and refrigerate overnight (at least 8 hours).
3. In the morning, top with toasted walnuts for added protein and texture. Add honey and fresh fruit. Love it? YES!

Scrambled Eggs, Kalamata Olives & Tomatoes

COOK: 15 MINS I SERVES: 1 I CAL: 425 KCAL

Ingredients

- 2 large eggs
- 1/4 cup chopped Kalamata olives
  (or any available black olives you have)
- 1/4 cup chopped cherry tomatoes
- 1/4 cup crumbled feta cheese
- 1 tbsp chopped fresh oregano
- 1 tbsp olive oil, salt and pepper to taste

Instructions:

1. In a bowl, combine your eggs (whisk together) with a sprinkle of salt and pepper. Heat olive oil in a skillet over medium heat. Add Kalamata olives and cherry tomatoes and saute the tomatoes until they start to wrinkle slightly.
2. Pour in the egg mixture and scramble with a spatula until almost set.
3. Stir in feta cheese and oregano. Simmer for another minute or until warmed all the way through. Serve warm with crusty bread. It's a taste sensation that'll leave you wanting more.

Frittata with Roasted Vegetables & Feta

COOK: 25 MINS I SERVES: 4 I CAL: 350 KCAL

Ingredients

Frittata:
- 8 eggs (beaten)
- 1/4 cup milk
- 1/4 cup feta (crumbled)
- 1/2 cup spinach (chopped)
- 1/4 cup parsley (chopped)
- 1/4 tsp dried oregano
- pinch red pepper flakes (optional)
- salt & pepper
- 1 tbsp olive oil

Roasted Veggies:
- 1 tbsp olive oil
- 1 zucchini (diced)
- 1 red bell pepper (diced)
- 1 yellow bell pepper (diced)
- 1/2 red onion (sliced)
- salt & pepper

Instructions:

1. Preheat oven to 400°F (200°C). Toss veggies with olive oil, salt & pepper. Roast 15-20 mins until tender-crisp.
2. Whisk eggs, milk, feta, spinach, parsley, oregano, red pepper flakes (if using), salt & pepper.
3. Heat 1 tbsp olive oil in an oven-safe skillet over medium heat. Pour in egg mixture, swirl to distribute. Cook a few minutes until edges set.
4. Fold in the roasted veggies. Transfer the skillet to the oven and bake for 15- 20 minutes, or until the center is set.
5. Cool slightly, slice. Garnish with some fresh herbs for extra flair if you're feeling fancy. This is hot, this is happening, this is a taste bud adventure that'll leave you wanting more. So grab a plate, grab a fork, and get ready to devour!

Caprese Frittata with Fresh Basil

COOK: 20 MINS I SERVES: 1 I CAL: 300 KCAL

Ingredients

- 2 large eggs
- 1/4 cup shredded mozzarella cheese
- 1/4 cup chopped cherry tomatoes
- 1 tbsp chopped fresh basil
- 1/4 tsp dried oregano
- Pinch of salt and pepper
- 1 tbsp olive oil

Instructions:

1. In a bowl, whisk together eggs, 1/2 shredded mozzarella cheese, chopped tomatoes, and fresh basil. Season with oregano, salt, pepper.
2. Get your non-stick pan nice and hot with a swirl of olive oil. Pour in the egg mixture.
3. Cook for 5-7 minutes, or until the bottom starts to set.
4. Scatter the leftover mozzarella cheese over the surface.
5. Cover the pan and cook for another 2-3 minutes, or until fully set through.
6. Slide the cooked frittata onto a plate and enjoy warm. Delicious!

Italian Sausage & Scrambled Eggs with Spinach

COOK: 15 MINS I SERVES: 1 I CAL: 660 KCAL

Ingredients

- 2 large eggs
- 2 mild Italian sausage links, casings removed and crumbled
- 1/2 cup chopped fresh spinach
- 1/4 cup shredded Parmesan cheese
- 1 tbsp chopped fresh parsley
- 1/4 tsp dried oregano
- Pinch of salt and pepper
- 1 tbsp olive oil

Instructions:

1. Heat olive oil in a pan over medium heat. Add crumbled Italian sausage (Look for lighter or turkey Italian sausage links to reduce fat content and calories) and cook until browned, about 5 minutes. Drain excess grease.
2. Push the sausage to one side of the pan and add more olive oil if your pan seems dry.
3. Whisk together eggs, oregano, salt, and pepper in a bowl. Gently tip the egg mixture into the empty space beside the sausage. As the eggs begin to set, gently scramble them with a spatula.
4. Stir in chopped fresh spinach and cook for another minute, or until wilted.
5. Sprinkle with Parmesan cheese and fresh parsley before serving. Serve with the cooked Italian sausage.

Couscous Salad with Herbs & Vegetables

COOK: 15 MINS I SERVES: 1 I CAL: 320 KCAL

Ingredients

- 1 cup Israeli couscous (pearl couscous)
- 1 cup chopped cucumber
- 1/2 cup chopped cherry tomatoes
- 1/4 cup chopped red onion
- 1/4 cup chopped fresh parsley
- 1/4 cup chopped fresh mint
- 2 tbsp olive oil
- 1 tbsp lemon juice
- 1/4 tsp salt
- Pinch of black pepper
- 1 slice whole wheat bread, toasted (if you want to do a toast)

Instructions:

1. In a saucepan, cook Israeli couscous according to package directions. Drain and fluff with a fork.
2. While couscous cooks, combine chopped cucumber, red onion, cherry tomatoes, mint and parsley in a large bowl.
3. Serve as a salat or spread the couscous salad on the toasted bread. There you have it, sunshine on a plate! Now get stuck in, like nobody's watching.

Sweet Spiced Carrot Scramble & Toasted Pita

COOK: 15 MINS I SERVES: 1 I CAL: 330 KCAL

Ingredients

- 2 large eggs
- 1/2 cup grated carrots
- 1/4 cup chopped red onion
- 1 tbsp chopped fresh cilantro
- 1/2 tsp ground cinnamon
- Pinch of ground ginger
- 1/4 tsp ground cumin
- Salt and pepper to taste
- 1 tbsp olive oil
- 1 whole wheat pita bread

Instructions:

1. In a small bowl, whisk together eggs with salt and pepper. Start by heating olive oil in a pan over medium heat. Then, add the red onion and cook it for about 2 minutes, or until it softens.
2. Stir in grated carrots and spices (cinnamon, ginger, cumin). Cook for another minute, allowing the flavors to bloom.
3. Pour in the egg mixture and scramble until cooked through. Stir in fresh cilantro just before serving.
4. Toast a whole wheat pita bread in a dry skillet or toaster. Serve the scrambled eggs on top of the toasted pita for a satisfying breakfast. Fresh, vibrant, and ready to tantalize your taste buds.

Sweet Potato Pancakes with Maple Syrup & Nuts

COOK: 15 MINS I SERVES: 2-3 PANCAKES I CAL: 370 KCAL

Ingredients

- 1 cup mashed sweet potato (roasted or microwaved)
- 1/2 cup rolled oats
- 1/4 cup milk (dairy or non-dairy)
- 1 egg
- 1/2 tsp ground cinnamon
- 1/4 tsp ground ginger
- Pinch of sea salt
- Maple syrup or honey and chopped pecans (for serving)
- Cooking spray

Instructions:

1. In a bowl, mash the sweet potato together until smooth.
2. Stir in rolled oats, milk, egg, cinnamon, ginger, and salt. Mix well to form a thick batter.
3. Heat a lightly oiled pan or griddle over medium heat. Spray the pan with cooking spray.
4. Pour batter into small circles, forming pancakes. Cook for 2-3 minutes per side or until golden brown.
5. Serve warm, drizzled with maple syrup and topped with chopped pecans. Almost as good as you.

Honey-Almond Ricotta Pancakes & Berries

COOK: 15 MINS I SERVES: 4-5 PANCAKES I CAL: 450 KCAL

Ingredients

- 1 cup ricotta cheese
- 1/2 cup all-purpose flour (or whole wheat flour)
- 2 large eggs
- 1/4 cup milk (dairy or non-dairy)
- 2 tbsp honey
- 1 tsp baking powder
- 1/4 tsp ground cinnamon
- Pinch of salt
- 1/4 cup sliced almonds
- Fresh berries (for serving)
- Maple syrup (optional)

Instructions:

1. In a bowl, whisk together eggs, milk, honey, ricotta cheese, baking powder, cinnamon, and salt.
2. Stir in flour until just combined. Don't overmix. Fold in sliced almonds.
3. Heat a lightly oiled pan or griddle over medium heat. Spray with cooking spray.
4. Pour batter into small circles, forming pancakes. Cook for 2-3 minutes per side or until golden brown.
5. Serve warm with fresh berries and a drizzle of maple syrup (optional). Now go forth and conquer the kitchen, kitchen hero!

APPETIZERS & SALADS

Zucchini Fritters

Tip: Drain any excess moisture from the grated zucchini for crispier fritters. If needed, use a non-stick pan to prevent sticking.

COOK: 20 MINS I SERVES: 10-12 FR. I CAL: 90 KCAL (1 FR.)

Ingredients

- 1 medium zucchini, grated
- 1/4 cup crumbled feta cheese (optional)
- 1/4 cup chopped fresh dill or parsley
- 1 egg, beaten
- 1/4 cup chickpea flour (or all-purpose flour)
- 1 tbsp olive oil
- Salt and pepper to taste
- yogurt to dip

Instructions:

1. Grate the zucchini, then wring out any extra liquid using a clean paper towel.
2. In a bowl, combine zucchini, cheese (if using), herbs, flour, egg, olive oil, salt, and pepper. Mix well.
3. Get a pan going over medium heat with a drizzle of oil. Spoon out batter for each fritter.
4. Cook for 2-3 minutes per side or until golden brown and crispy.
5. Let excess oil drip off on paper towels for a few minutes and serve warm. Serve with a yogurt dip or tzatziki.

Tzatziki

Tip: Use a strainer to remove excess liquid from the grated cucumber for a thicker (better) tzatziki.

COOK: 10 MINS I SERVES: 1 CUP I CAL: 30 KCAL (2 TBSP)

Ingredients

- 1 cup plain Greek yogurt
- 1/2 cucumber, grated and squeezed dry
- 1 tbsp olive oil
- 1 clove garlic, minced
- 1 tbsp fresh dill, chopped
- Salt and pepper to taste

Instructions:

1. In a bowl, combine yogurt, grated cucumber (strain the grated cucumber over a bowl to remove excess moisture), olive oil, garlic, dill, salt, and pepper.
2. Stir well and refrigerate for at least 30 minutes to allow flavors to develop.
3. Serve chilled with pita bread, vegetables (fresh or grilled/roasted), meat, fish, or as a dip for appetizers.

Whipped Feta with Roasted Peppers & Herbs

Tip: Substitute sun-dried tomatoes for roasted red peppers for a different flavor twist.

COOK: 10 MINS I SERVES: 1 CUP I CAL: 120 KCAL (2 TBSP)

Ingredients

- 1/2 cup crumbled feta cheese
- 1/4 cup roasted red peppers, chopped (from jar or roasted yourself)
- 2 tbsp olive oil
- 1 tbsp fresh parsley, chopped
- 1 tbsp fresh mint, chopped (optional)
- Pinch of dried oregano
- Pinch of red pepper flakes (optional)
- Salt and pepper to taste
- Garlic if you like (1-2 cloves)

Instructions:

1. In a food processor, combine feta cheese, roasted red peppers, olive oil, parsley, mint (if using), oregano, red pepper flakes (if using), salt, and pepper. Add garlic if you like.
2. Blend until smooth and creamy. To make the dip smoother, add a splash of water or milk while blending.
3. Serve with pita bread, vegetables (fresh or roasted/grilled), or crackers.

Spicy Shrimp with Garlic & Lemon

COOK: 20 MINS I SERVES: 2 I CAL: 200 KCAL PER SERVING

Ingredients

- 1/2 lb fresh shrimp, peeled and deveined
- 1 tbsp olive oil
- 2 cloves garlic, minced
- 1/2 tsp red pepper flakes (adjust for spice preference)
- 1/4 cup dry white wine (optional)
- Juice of 1/2 lemon
- Fresh parsley (chopped, for garnish)

Instructions:

1. Heat olive oil in a large skillet over medium heat. Cook the shrimp until they turn a lovely shade of pink and opaque, about 2-3 minutes per side.
2. Add garlic and red pepper flakes, cook for 30 seconds, stirring constantly.
3. Deglaze the pan with white wine (if using), scraping up any browned bits. Let simmer for 1 minute.
4. Add a squeeze of lemon juice for a touch of brightness, then simmer until the sauce thickens slightly.
5. Garnish with fresh parsley. Serve with crusty bread for dipping in the sauce.

Bruschetta with Tomatoes, Basil, Balsamic Glaze

Tip: Rub the toasted bread with a garlic clove for extra flavor before adding the topping.

COOK: 15 MINS I SERVES: 4 I CAL: 170 KCAL PER SERVING

Ingredients

- 1 baguette, sliced diagonally into 1/2 inch thick pieces
- 1 tbsp olive oil
- 2 large tomatoes, seeded and diced
- 1/4 cup chopped fresh basil
- 1/2 mozarella
- Salt and pepper to taste
- Balsamic glaze (store-bought or homemade)

Instructions:

1. Preheat oven to broiler setting. Brush baguette slices with olive oil and toast under the broiler for 2-3 minutes per side, or until golden brown.
2. In a bowl, combine diced tomatoes, basil, salt, and pepper.
3. Top toasted bread slices with mozarella slices (pepper and salt before) and the tomato mixture. Drizzle with balsamic glaze.

Mini Spanakopita Bites

COOK: 20 MINS I SERVES: 12 BITES I CAL: 55 KCAL (1 B.)

Ingredients

- 1 sheet frozen phyllo dough, thawed
- 1/4 cup olive oil, melted
- 1 cup chopped spinach
- 1/4 cup crumbled feta cheese
- 1/4 cup chopped red onion
- 1 egg, beaten
- Salt and pepper to taste

Instructions:

1. Preheat oven to 400°F (200°C). Lightly grease a baking sheet.
2. In a bowl, combine chopped spinach, feta cheese, red onion, egg, salt, and pepper.
3. Thaw phyllo dough according to package instructions. Lightly oil a sheet of phyllo dough.
4. Place a small spoonful of the spinach filling at one end of the dough sheet. Create a triangular shape by lifting the dough sheet and folding it over the filling, meeting the opposite side of the dough. Continue folding diagonally down the length of the dough, creating a triangular pastry. Repeat with remaining phyllo dough and filling. Brush the tops of the spanakopita bites with olive oil.
5. Bake for 15-20 minutes. Now, get ready to impress your dinner guests (or yourself!).

Grilled Eggplant Stacks with Tomato, Mozzarella

COOK: 25 MINS I SERVES: 2 I CAL: 300 KCAL PER SERVING

Ingredients

- 1 small eggplant, sliced into 1/2 inch thick rounds
- 1 tbsp olive oil
- 1 large tomato, sliced
- 4 oz mozzarella cheese, sliced
- Fresh basil leaves (for garnish)
- Salt and pepper to taste

Instructions:

1. Preheat a grill pan or grill to medium heat. Brush eggplant slices with olive oil.
2. Grill eggplant slices for 2-3 minutes per side, or until softened.
3. Layer grilled eggplant slices on a plate, top with tomato slices and mozzarella cheese.
4. Grill the assembled stacks for another 1-2 minutes, or until cheese melts.
5. Garnish with fresh basil leaves, salt, and pepper.

Stuffed Cherry Peppers with Goat Cheese, Herbs

COOK: 15 MINS I SERVES: 4 I CAL: 100 KCAL PER SERVING

Ingredients

- 12 large cherry peppers
- 4 oz goat cheese, crumbled
- 2 tbsp chopped fresh herbs (parsley, chives, dill)
- 1 tbsp olive oil
- Salt and pepper to taste

Instructions:

1. Preheat oven to 400°F (200°C).
2. Cut the tops off the cherry peppers and remove seeds and membranes.
3. In a bowl, combine crumbled goat cheese, chopped herbs, olive oil, salt, and pepper.
4. Stuff the pepper halves with the goat cheese mixture.
5. Place stuffed peppers on a baking sheet and bake for 10-15 minutes, or until peppers are softened and filling is warmed through.

Spiced Chickpea Fritters & Lemon Yogurt Sauce

Tip: Don't be afraid to experiment with different herbs in the sauce. Fresh mint or chives could be a delicious substitution for the dill.

COOK: 25 MINS I SERVES: 4 I CAL: 260 KCAL PER SERVING

Ingredients

- 1 can (15 oz) chickpeas, drained and rinsed
- 1/4 cup chopped red onion
- 1/4 cup chopped fresh parsley
- 1 clove garlic, minced
- 1/2 tsp chili powder (optional)
- 1/4 cup all-purpose flour (or gluten-free alternative)
- 1 tsp ground cumin
- 1 egg, beaten
- Olive oil for frying

Lemon Yogurt Sauce:
- 1/2 cup Greek yogurt,
- 1 tbsp lemon juice
- 1 tbsp chopped dill, salt & pepper

Instructions:

1. Pulse chickpeas, veggies, spices in a food processor (coarse, not smooth). Mix with flour, egg, salt, pepper. If the fritter batter seems too loose, add a tablespoon more of flour until it reaches a consistency that holds its shape when spooned.
2. Heat oil in a pan over medium heat. Scoop 2 tbsp batter per fritter, flatten slightly. Cook 2-3 mins per side until golden brown.
3. Whisk yogurt, lemon juice, dill, salt, pepper for the sauce.
4. Serve warm fritters with a dollop of sauce!

Fig, Prosciutto Skewers with Balsamic Reduction

COOK: 10 MINS I SERVES: 4 I CAL: 200 KCAL PER SERVING

Ingredients

- 8 fresh figs, cut in half
- 8 slices prosciutto
- 1 tbsp olive oil
- 1/4 cup balsamic vinegar
- 1 tbsp brown sugar (optional)

Instructions:

1. Thread fig halves and prosciutto slices alternately onto skewers.
2. Heat olive oil in a skillet over medium heat. Sear the skewers for 1-2 minutes per side, or until prosciutto is slightly crisp.
3. In a small saucepan, combine balsamic vinegar and brown sugar (if using). Bring to a simmer and cook for 5-7 minutes, or until thickened slightly.
4. Drizzle balsamic reduction over the fig and prosciutto skewers before serving.

Green Asparagus with Tomatoes & Parmesan

Tip: Feeling adventurous? Introduce a touch of garlicky goodness by adding a minced garlic clove to the pan along with the olive oil while cooking the asparagus.

COOK: 20 MINS I SERVES: 2 I CAL: 150 KCAL PER SERVING

Ingredients

- 12-15 green asparagus spears (Choose similar-thickness asparagus for even cooking)
- 1 tbsp olive oil
- 8-10 cherry tomatoes
- Salt and freshly ground black pepper, to taste
- oregano (optional)
- 2 tbsps grated Parmesan cheese
- garlic clove (optional)
- fresh lemon juice

Instructions:

1. Preheat oven to 200°C.
2. Wash, trim, and snap asparagus ends. Toss with olive oil, salt, oregano and pepper in a bowl.
3. Line a baking sheet with parchment paper. Spread asparagus in a single layer and roast for 8-10 minutes.
4. Remove pan, add tomatoes, and roast for an additional 2-3 minutes.
5. Serve hot with Parmesan cheese.
6. Drizzle with lemon juice for a brighter flavor.

Grilled Calamari with Lemon & Herbs

COOK: 15 MINS I SERVES: 2 I CAL: 200 KCAL PER SERVING

Ingredients

- 1 pound fresh calamari, cleaned and cut into rings
- 1 tbsp olive oil
- Juice of 1 lemon
- 1 or 2 garlic cloves, chopped
- 1 tsp chopped fresh parsley
- 1/2 tsp dried oregano
- Salt and pepper to taste

Instructions:

1. Preheat a grill pan or grill to medium-high heat.
2. In a bowl, toss calamari rings with olive oil, lemon juice, parsley, chopped garlic cloves, oregano, salt, and pepper.
3. Grill the calamari for 2-3 minutes per side or until opaque and cooked through. Be careful not to overcook, as calamari can become tough.
4. Serve calamari rings with tzatziki. You will love it!

Protein Bean Tacos with Avocado Guacamole

It may not be considered a traditional Mediterranean dish, but it perfectly embodies the philosophy of Mediterranean cuisine: fresh, vegetable-based, and absolutely delicious!

Tip: Get creative with your protein! Leftover grilled chicken or fish would also be delicious and add a Mediterranean touch.

Meatless: Don't have TVP? No problem! Use another ½ can of refried or crumbled cooked black beans for extra protein.

Guacamole. Brown Away Blues: To prevent browning, you can place the avocado pit in the husk. However, it's best to enjoy guacamole fresh for the most vibrant flavor. Spice it Up! Add more jalapeno pepper or a pinch of cayenne pepper for a spicier kick.

COOK: 30 MINS | SERVES: 6 | CAL: 250 - 350 PER TACO

Ingredients

The Base:
- 6 tortillas (flour, corn, whole wheat - you pick!)
- 1 can refried beans (Homemade rocks!)

The Protein Powerhouse (choose your favorite):
- Shredded leftover chicken or turkey (about 1 cup)
- Ground tempeh or lentils, seasoned and cooked (about 1 cup)
- Crispy tofu crumbles (about 1 cup)
- **OR** go meatless with an extra 1/2 can of refried beans and 1/4 cup crumbled TVP (textured vegetable protein)

The Fresh Fiesta:
- 2 ripe avocados
- 1 cup fresh sprouts (mung bean, lentil, or a mix!)
- 1/2 cup chopped fresh cilantro, 1 cup cherry tomatoes, halved
- The Wildcard (optional): 1/4 cup kimchi (for a spicy kick!)

Favorite Guacamole (optional):
- 2 ripe avocados, halved, pitted, and scooped (choose avocados that give a little when you press them gently, but aren't mushy)
- 1/4 cup chopped red onion
- 1 tbsp fresh lime juice
- 4-5 cherry tomatoes
- 1/4 cup chopped fresh cilantro (don't waste coriander stems! Chop finely and add to dish for extra flavor)
- 1 jalapeno pepper, seeded and minced (optional, for a kick of spice)
- Salt and freshly ground black pepper to taste
- 3-4 garlic clove or garlic powder
- A dollop of sour cream for a richer taste (for an extra creamy touch)

Instructions:

1. Warm those tortillas! Preheat your oven to 300°F (150°C). Wrap the tortillas in foil or place them in a single layer on a baking sheet. Warm them in the oven for 3-5 minutes or until slightly softened and pliable.
2. Heat up the Beans: In a small pan over medium heat, warm your refried beans until hot and bubbly. Season with a pinch of salt and pepper if desired.
3. Prep the fiesta: Wash and chop your fresh ingredients - the sprouts, cilantro, and cherry tomatoes.
4. Guacamole time! Make your favorite guacamole recipe using the avocados. Here's a quick suggestion: mash the avocados with a squeeze of lime juice, chopped garlic, fresh cilantro, tomatoes, a pinch of salt, pepper, jalapeno pepper, a dollop of sour cream. Set aside some guacamole for garnish.
5. Assemble your Taco Dreams! Now comes the fun part! Take your warmed tortillas and spread a layer of refried beans on each. Add your chosen protein, followed by the fresh fiesta of sprouts, cilantro, and tomatoes. Top it all off with a generous dollop of guacamole. Are you feeling adventurous? Add a sprinkle of kimchi for a spicy surprise!

Roasted Garlic Hummus

Tip: Herb Variations. Feel free to experiment with different herb combinations to suit your taste. Mint, dill, chives, and oregano are all great options to use alone or combine.

COOK: 30 MINS I SERVES: 4-6 I CAL: 200 KCAL

Ingredients

- 1 (15-ounce) can chickpeas, drained and rinsed
- 1 head garlic
- 1/4 cup tahini (sesame seed paste)
- 2 tbsps fresh lemon juice
- 2 tbsps olive oil
- 1/4 cup water (more as needed)
- 1/2 tsp ground cumin
- 1/4 tsp sea salt
- Pinch of cayenne pepper (optional)
- Extra virgin olive oil, for drizzling (optional)
- Fresh parsley for garnish

Instructions:

1. Roast the Garlic: Preheat oven to 400°F (200°C). Cut off the top 1/4 inch of the garlic head to expose the cloves. To lock in moisture and flavor, coat with olive oil and enclose tightly in aluminum foil. Roast for 20-25 minutes or until cloves are soft and golden brown. Let cool slightly. For a smoky flavored hummus, roast the chickpeas and garlic for the last 10 minutes of roasting time. Spread chickpeas on a baking sheet, drizzle with olive oil and season with salt and pepper before roasting.
2. Combine Ingredients: In a food processor, combine chickpeas, roasted garlic cloves (squeezed from their skins), tahini, lemon juice, olive oil, water, cumin, salt, and cayenne pepper (if using). Continue processing until completely smooth and homogenous, scraping down the sides as needed. Add water, 1 tablespoon at a time, to achieve desired consistency. Serve: Transfer hummus to a serving bowl. Drizzle with additional olive oil and sprinkle with fresh parsley (optional) for garnish. Serve with pita bread, vegetables, or crackers.

Roasted Asparagus in Flaky Pastry

Tip: Feel free to swap the oregano for other dried herbs like thyme, rosemary, or a pinch of red pepper flakes for some heat.

COOK: 25 MINS I SERVES: 9 I CAL: 150 KCAL PER SERVING

Ingredients

- 1 sheet puff pastry (thawed)
- 3 tbsp olive oil
- 2 bundles of asparagus (trimmed)
- 1/2 cup feta, crumbled
- 1/4 cup sun-dried tomatoes (chopped)
- 1 egg yolk (beaten)
- 1/2 tsp dried oregano
- 1/4 tsp salt
- 1/4 tsp freshly ground black pepper

Instructions:

1. Combine the trimmed asparagus, oregano, salt, pepper and olive oil in a large bowl. Arrange the seasoned asparagus in an even layer across a baking sheet. Roast for 10-12 minutes, or until tender-crisp.
2. Unfold the puff pastry and cut it into squares (9 pieces). Drizzle the puffed pastry with olive oil.
3. Top squares with asparagus, feta, and tomatoes.
4. Brush edges with egg yolk, fold into triangles and seal. Give the bundles another oil and garlic sprinkle. Brush tops with remaining egg yolk.
5. Bake at 400°F (200°C) for 15-20 minutes or until golden brown.

Spicy Greek Feta Dip

COOK: 10 MINS | SERVES: 4 | CAL: 150 KCAL PER SERVING

Ingredients

- 8 oz crumbled feta
- 1/2 cup roasted red pepper (store-bought or roasted)
- 1 jalapeno (seeded, adjust for spice)
- 1 garlic clove, minced
- 2 tbsp olive oil
- 1 tbsp red wine vinegar
- 1/4 tsp dried oregano
- Pinch red pepper flakes (optional)
- Salt & pepper

Instructions:

1. Toss that crumbled feta into your food processor and give it a few pulses until it's broken down into lovely, tiny pieces.
2. Now it's party time! Add the jalapeno (remember, you control the spice!), roasted red pepper, garlic, olive oil, red wine vinegar, and oregano to the feta party in the food processor. Blend it all on high until it's smooth and creamy – a delicious symphony of flavors!
3. Transfer your masterpiece to a shallow dish or bowl. Get creative with fresh parsley, Kalamata olives, leftover feta, and a sprinkle of chopped roasted red pepper. Don't forget an extra drizzle of olive oil for good measure. Serve with toasted pita bread.

Crispy Garlic Parmesan Brussels Sprouts

Tip: You can try broccoli spears instead of Brussels sprouts as well.

COOK: 25 MINS | SERVES: 4 | CAL: 120 KCAL PER SERVING

Ingredients

- 1 pound Brussels sprouts, trimmed and halved (
- 1 tbsp olive oil
- 1/2 tsp garlic powder
- 1/2 tsp salt
- 1/2 tsp black pepper
- 1/2 cup grated Parmesan cheese
- Fresh parsley, chopped (optional, for garnish)

Instructions:

1. Preheat oven to 400°F (200°C). Wash, trim, and halve Brussels sprouts.
2. Trim, halve or quarter depending on size, then toss in a bowl with olive oil, garlic powder, salt, and pepper.
3. Spread on a baking sheet and roast for 15-18 minutes or until golden brown and crispy, shaking halfway through. Out of the oven, then a shower of Parmesan. Let sit 1-2 minutes to melt cheese.
4. Garnish with parsley (optional) and serve hot!

Greek Roasted Beet Salad & Goat / Feta Cheese

COOK: 30 MINS I SERVES: 1 I CAL: 300 KCAL

Ingredients

For the Roasted Beets:
- 1 small red beet, peeled and thinly sliced
- 1 small golden beet, peeled and thinly sliced
- 1 tsp olive oil
- 1/4 tsp garlic powder
- 1/4 tsp onion powder
- Pinch of salt, pinch of black pepper

For the Salad:
- 1/2 cup baby arugula
- 1 tbsp walnuts, finely chopped
- 1 ounce crumbled goat cheese or feta cheese
- 1 tbsp pomegranate arils (optional)

For the Lemon Yogurt Dressing:
- 1/4 cup plain Greek yogurt
- 1/2 tsp honey
- 1/2 tsp grated garlic
- 1 tbsp lemon juice
- Pinch of salt
- Pinch of black pepper

Instructions:

1. Preheat Oven: Set your oven to 400°F (200°C).
2. Roast the Beets: Combine the sliced beets with olive oil, garlic powder, onion powder, salt, and pepper in a bowl. Toss to coat. Spread the seasoned beets on a baking sheet and roast for 15-20 minutes, or until tender-crisp (flipping them halfway through). Use pre-cooked or pre-sliced beets to save time.
3. Prepare the Dressing: While the beets roast, whisk together Greek yogurt, honey, garlic, lemon juice, salt, and pepper in a small bowl.
4. Assemble the Salad: Arrange the baby arugula on a plate. Top with roasted beets, chopped walnuts, crumbled goat cheese (or feta), and pomegranate arils (if using). Dress & Enjoy: Drizzle the lemon yogurt dressing over the salad and enjoy!

Classic Greek Salad

COOK: 15 MINS I SERVES: 1 I CAL: 250 KCAL

Ingredients

- 1 tomato, cut into large cubes
- 1/2 cup chopped cucumber cut into large chunks
- 1/2 green bell pepper, cut into large pieces (smooth green bell pepper; only this pepper is used in an authentic Greek salad
- 1/4 cup crumbled feta cheese
- 5 Kalamata olives, pitted and halved (or any available black olives you have)
- 2 tbsps chopped red onion
- 1 tbsp olive oil
- 1 tbsp red wine vinegar
- Pinch of dried oregano
- Salt, freshly ground black pepper

Instructions:

1. Combine the cubed tomatoes, cucumber chunks, feta cheese, red onion, bell pepper, and olives in a large bowl. Use high-quality ingredients for the best flavor. Vine-ripened tomatoes, flavorful cucumbers, and briny Kalamata olives will make all the difference.
2. In a separate small bowl, whisk together red wine vinegar, the olive oil, and oregano. Dress the salad by pouring on the dressing and tossing to combine. Season with salt and pepper to taste. Serve immediately, enjoy!

Arugula, Nuts & Goat Cheese Salad

Tip: You can use strawberries, pears, red grapes or any other berries instead of peaches. You can also use Italian buratta cheese instead of goat cheese.

COOK: 20 MINS I SERVES: 1 I CAL: 270 KCAL

Ingredients

- 2 cups baby arugula, washed and dried
- 2 oz crumbled goat cheese
- 1 giant peach (sliced)
- 1 tbsp balsamic vinegar
- 1 tbsp olive oil
- handful of chopped walnuts or pecans.
- Salt and freshly ground black pepper to taste

Instructions:

1. While you wash and dry your arugula, measure out your goat cheese, and slice the peach. You can roast the peach for aroma for 10-12 minutes, or until slightly softened and golden brown. Toss peach slices with a drizzle of olive oil and a pinch of cinnamon (optional) before roasting them.
2. Place the arugula on a plate. Crumble the goat cheese evenly over the arugula. Scatter the sliced peach on top. Add the nuts.
3. Dressing Magic: In a small bowl, whisk together the balsamic vinegar and olive oil. For more sweetness use apple balsamic vinegar. Season with a pinch of salt and pepper to taste. Drizzle the dressing over the salad. Serve & enjoy this refreshing and flavorful salad on its own or pair it with grilled chicken or fish.

Lentil Salad with Sun-Dried Tomatoes & Herbs

COOK: 20 MINS I SERVES: 1 I CAL: 300 KCAL

Ingredients

- 1/2 cup cooked lentils (brown, green, or black lentils work well)
- 1/4 cup chopped sun-dried tomatoes (not packed in oil)
- 1 tbsp chopped fresh herbs (parsley, arugula, basil, or a mix)
- 1/4 avocado, diced
- 1 tbsp crumbled feta cheese
- 1 tbsp balsamic vinegar
- 1 tbsp olive oil
- Salt and freshly ground black pepper, to taste

Instructions:

1. While you gather your ingredients, cook your lentils according to the package instructions if they are not already cooked. Dice the avocado and chop the sun-dried tomatoes and fresh herbs.
2. Assemble the Salad: In a bowl, unite the lentils, sun-dried tomatoes, and fresh herbs.
3. Whisk together the balsamic vinegar and olive oil in a separate small bowl. Season with salt and pepper. Drizzle the dressing over the lentil salad.
4. Optional Feta: If desired, sprinkle the crumbled feta cheese on top of the salad for an extra creaminess and salty flavor.
5. Serve & Savor! Enjoy this refreshing and protein-rich salad or pair it with whole-wheat pita bread.

Quinoa Nuts Salad with Roasted Vegetables

COOK: 25 MINS I SERVES: 1 I CAL: 350 KCAL

Ingredients

- 1/4 cup uncooked quinoa, rinsed
- 1/2 cup chopped vegetables (mix and match! Options include bell peppers, zucchini, cherry tomatoes, red onion)
- 1 tbsp olive oil
- 1/4 tsp dried oregano
- Salt and freshly ground black pepper to taste

For Garnish (optional):
- 1 tbsp crumbled feta cheese
- 1 tbsp chopped walnuts or pecans
- Fresh parsley sprig

Instructions:

1. Rinse your quinoa thoroughly. Wash and chop your chosen vegetables into bite-sized pieces. Feel free to experiment with different vegetables! Broccoli florets, asparagus spears, or eggplant cubes can also be delicious additions.
2. Heat oven to 400°F (200°C). Toss your chopped vegetables with olive oil, oregano, salt, and pepper in a large bowl. Spread on a baking sheet in a single layer. Roast 15 min. or until tender-crisp.
3. Combine the rinsed quinoa with ½ cup water (or follow package instructions for single serving). Bring to a boil, then reduce heat, cover, and simmer for 12-15 minutes (until the quinoa is fluffy and the water is absorbed. Fluff the quinoa with a fork once the vegetables are roasted and the quinoa is cooked. In a bowl, combine the roasted vegetables and cooked quinoa.
4. Garnish Magic: For an extra touch of flavor and texture, top your salad with crumbled feta cheese, chopped walnuts, and a fresh parsley sprig. From my kitchen to yours, with love (and a lot of flavor). Now get cooking!

Tuna Salad with White Beans & Artichokes

COOK: 20 MINS I SERVES: 1 I CAL: 300 KCAL

Ingredients

- 2 oz canned tuna in water, drained and flaked
- 1/2 cup canned white beans (cannellini, great Northern, or chickpeas all work!) - rinsed and drained
- 2-3 quartered marinated artichoke hearts (jarred)
- 1 tbsp chopped fresh parsley
- 1 tbsp chopped red onion (optional)
- 1 tbsp olive oil
- 1 tbsp lemon juice
- Salt and freshly ground black pepper to taste

Instructions:

1. While you drain your tuna and rinse your white beans, chop the red onion and parsley (if using).
2. In a bowl, combine the flaked tuna, white beans, artichoke hearts, red onion (if using), and chopped parsley.
3. To create the dressing, whisk olive oil and lemon juice together in a separate, small bowl. Season with a pinch of salt and pepper to taste.
4. Toss & Serve: Drizzle the dressing over the salad ingredients and toss gently to combine. Enjoy this light and flavorful appetizer or pair it with whole-wheat crackers or pita bread for a satisfying snack.

Summer Quinoa Salad with Feta & Mint

Tip: Power up your salad with protein-packed chickpeas or lentils for sustained energy. For an added health kick, sprinkle some red pepper flakes into your dressing for a metabolism boost!

COOK: 20 MINS I SERVES: 1 I CAL: 300 KCAL

Ingredients

- 1/4 cup uncooked quinoa, rinsed
- 1/4 cup chopped cucumber
- 1/2 cup chopped cherry tomatoes
- 1/4 cup crumbled feta cheese
- 2 tbsps chopped fresh mint
- 1 tbsp olive oil
- 1 tbsp lemon juice
- Pinch of salt and freshly ground black pepper

Instructions:

1. Rinse your quinoa according to package instructions. While it's rinsing, chop your cucumber, tomatoes, and fresh mint.
2. Follow the package instructions to cook your rinsed quinoa. Generally, it will require simmering in 1/2 cup of water for about 10 minutes, or until fluffy and cooked through.
3. Once the quinoa is cooked and cooled slightly, fluff it with a fork and transfer it to a bowl. Add the chopped cucumber, tomatoes, fresh mint.
4. In a small bowl, whisk together the olive oil and lemon juice. Season with
5. a pinch of salt and pepper to taste. Drizzle the dressing over the salad.
6. Top your salad with the crumbled feta cheese for a creamy and salty touch. That's how easy and delicious this dish is!

Asparagus Feta Salad with Pistachios & Lemon

Tip: Grill asparagus for a char. Substitute nuts & cheese. Add honey/agave for sweetness.

COOK: 20 MINS I SERVES: 1 I CAL: 220 KCAL

Ingredients

- 5-6 asparagus spears, trimmed
- 1/4 cup crumbled feta cheese
- 1 tbsp chopped pistachios
- 1 tbsp olive oil
- 1 tablespoon lemon juice
- Salt and freshly ground black pepper, to taste

Instructions:

1. Wash asparagus, measure feta and pistachios. Cook asparagus (stovetop 3-4 min, microwave 2-3 min) until tender-crisp.
2. Arrange asparagus, crumble feta, sprinkle pistachios. Whisk olive oil, lemon juice, salt & pepper for dressing. Drizzle over salad.
3. Enjoy! Pair with grilled chicken/fish for a complete meal.

Shrimp Pasta Salad with Goat Cheese

COOK: 25 MINS I SERVES: 1 I CAL: 450 KCAL

Ingredients

- 4 oz shelled and deveined shrimp (thawed, patted dry)
- 1/2 cup cooked small pasta (fusilli, penne, or rotini)
- 1/4 cup drained and rinsed cannellini beans
- 2 tbsp chopped sun-dried tomatoes (not packed in oil)
- 2 tbsp crumbled goat cheese
- 1 tbsp chopped green olives
- 1 tbsp olive oil
- 1 tbsp fresh lemon juice
- 1/4 tsp dried oregano
- Salt and freshly ground black pepper to taste
- Fresh parsley (optional garnish)

Instructions:

1. While your pasta cooks according to package instructions, drain and rinse the cannellini beans. Chop the sun-dried tomatoes and green olives.
2. In a skillet, get your olive oil hot over medium heat. Then, toss your shrimp with salt and pepper to taste. Once the oil is shimmering, add the shrimp and cook for 2-3 minutes per side, looking for that opaque, pink color throughout. Take the pan off the heat and let the shrimp cool slightly before continuing.
3. In a bowl, combine the cooked pasta, cannellini beans, sun-dried tomatoes, and green olives.
4. In a small bowl, whisk together the lemon juice, oregano, and a pinch of salt and pepper. Drizzle this dressing over the salad and toss to coat.
5. Top the salad with the cooked shrimp and crumbled goat cheese. Garnish with fresh parsley (optional) and serve!

Orzo Salad with Cranberry Walnut Crumble

COOK: 25 MINS I SERVES: 1 I CAL: 420 KCAL

Ingredients

Cranberry Walnut Crumble:
- 1/4 cup cranberries (dried cranberries)
- 1 tbsp brown sugar
- 1 tbsp chopped walnuts
- Pinch of chili flakes (optional)

Salad:
- 1/2 cup dried orzo pasta, cooked according to package directions
- 1 cup chopped spinach
- 1/2 fennel bulb, thinly sliced
- 1/4 cup crumbled feta cheese
- 2 tbsps chopped olives (Castelvetrano)

Dressing:
- 1 tbsp olive oil
- 1/2 tsp dried oregano
- Salt, freshly ground black pepper
- 1 tbsp lemon juice
- 1 tbsp red wine vinegar
- 1 garlic clove, minced

Instructions:

1. Combine cranberries, brown sugar, walnuts, and chili flakes (if using) in a small bowl. Mix well and set aside.
2. In another small bowl, whisk together olive oil, oregano, salt, pepper, lemon juice, red wine vinegar, and minced garlic. Set aside. While the dressing and crumble are prepped, cook the orzo pasta according to package directions. Drain and rinse with cold water.
3. In a large bowl, combine the cooked orzo, chopped spinach, sliced fennel, crumbled feta cheese, and Castelvetrano olives (if using). Dress the salad by pouring on the dressing and tossing to coat. Top the salad with the prepared cranberry walnut crumble and enjoy!

Arugula Protein Salad with Veggies & Feta

COOK: 25 MINS I SERVES: 1 I CAL: 380 KCAL

Ingredients

- 2 cups arugula (washed & dried)
- 1/4 cup each: roasted sweet potato, chopped broccoli, steamed green beans (cut)
- 2 tbsp crumbled feta
- 1/4 cup chopped walnuts/pecans
- Protein: 2 oz grilled chicken (sliced) OR 1 oz crumbled salmon OR 1/4 cup cooked lentils
- 1 tbsp each: olive oil, lemon juice
- Salt & pepper

Instructions:

1. Wash arugula, chop veggies, cook protein.
2. In a bowl, combine your washed arugula, roasted veggies, crumbled feta, and chopped nuts. Top it all off with your champion protein of choice.
3. Whisk oil, lemon juice, salt & pepper. Drizzle over salad. Are you craving a tangier twist? Swap out the lemon juice for a splash of balsamic vinegar in your dressing.
4. Enjoy! Toss & savor the vibrant flavors.

Sun-Kissed Summer Salad with Burrata & Figs

COOK: 20 MINS I SERVES: 1 I CAL: 400 KCAL

Ingredients

- 1 ripe tomato, sliced
- 1 fresh fig, quartered
- 1/4 cup red onion, thinly sliced
- 1 tbsp capers, drained
- 1/2 ball fresh burrata cheese
- Fresh basil leaves, to taste
- 3 oz Prosciutto (optional)
- A few fresh mint leaves, to taste 1 tsp fig jam
- 1 tbsp olive oil
- Salt and freshly ground black pepper, to taste

Instructions:

1. Wash and slice your tomato. Quarter your fig. Thinly slice the red onion. Drain those capers. You're ready to assemble!
2. Arrange the sliced tomato and fig quarters on a plate. Scatter the red onion and capers over the top. Gently tear the fresh basil leaves and sprinkle them on the salad. Do the same with the mint leaves. Add Prosciutto.
3. Place the half ball of burrata cheese in the center of the salad. Let its creamy goodness be the star of the show!
4. In a small bowl, whisk together the olive oil and a pinch of salt and pepper. Drizzle this dressing over the salad.
5. If you're craving a touch of sweetness, drizzle a teaspoon of fig jam over the salad.

Greek Island Cabbage Salad

Tip: Craving more veggie good-ness? Add a diced cucumber or chopped tomato for a refreshing twist. For a heartier salad, add a grilled chicken breast or a handful of cooked chickpeas.

COOK: 15 MINS I SERVES: 1 I CAL: 200 KCAL

Ingredients

- 2 cups shredded green cabbage (about ½ head)
- 1/4 cup crumbled feta cheese
- 1/4 cup chopped black olives (Kalamata are perfect!)
- 1 tbsp fresh parsley, chopped (optional)
- 1 tbsp chopped red onion
- 1 tbsp olive oil
- 1 tbsp fresh lemon juice
- Salt and freshly ground black pepper, to taste

Instructions:

1. Wash and shred your cabbage – aim for thin strips for a delightful crunch. Roughly chop the olives, red onion, and parsley (if using).
2. In a large bowl, combine the shredded cabbage, chopped olives, crumbled feta and red onion. Sprinkle with fresh parsley for an extra pop of color and flavor (optional).
3. In a small bowl, whisk together the olive oil and fresh lemon juice. Season with a pinch of salt and pepper to taste. Drizzle this tangy dressing over your salad. Enjoy! Pair this salad with grilled chicken or fish for a complete Mediterranean-inspired meal.

Quinoa Mango Salad with Honey-Lime Vinaigrette

COOK: 25 MINS I SERVES: 1 I CAL: 350 KCAL

Ingredients

- 1/2 cup cooked quinoa (rinsed before cooking)
- 1/2 cup chopped ripe mango
- 1/2 cup diced red bell pepper
- 1/2 cup drained and rinsed black beans
- 1/4 cup chopped fresh cilantro

Honey-Lime-Dijon Dressing:
- 1 tbsp olive oil
- 1 tbsp fresh lime juice
- 1 tsp honey
- 1 tsp Dijon mustard
- Salt and freshly ground black pepper, to taste

Instructions:

1. While your quinoa cooks (if it hasn't already been prepared), gather your chopping skills! Dice the red bell pepper, chop the juicy mango, and rinse and drain the black beans. Cilantro lovers, chop up that fresh herb too!
2. In a bowl, combine the cooked quinoa, chopped mango, diced red pepper, and black beans. Top it all off with the fresh cilantro.
3. In a separate small bowl, whisk together the olive oil, lime juice, honey, and Dijon mustard. Season with a pinch of salt and pepper to taste. This is your tangy, sweet, and slightly spicy dressing magic!
4. Drizzle the delicious dressing over your salad creation, gently tossing everything together to coat it evenly. Enjoy!

Citrusy Red Cabbage Salad with Cheese & Nuts

Tip: Craving a creamier dressing? Swirl in a dollop of creamy Greek yogurt. Feeling adventurous? Throw in some sliced red onion for a bit of a bite.

COOK: 15 MINS I SERVES: 1 I CAL: 300 KCAL

Ingredients

- 2 cups thinly sliced red cabbage
- 1/4 cup chopped California Prunes
- 1/4 cup crumbled blue cheese (if you're not a fan, feta works too!)
- 1 tbsp chopped walnuts
- 2 tbsp fresh cilantro leaves

Citrus Dressing:
- 1 tbsp olive oil
- 1 tbsp lemon juice (freshly squeezed is best!)
- 1 tsp orange juice
- 1 tsp honey (or maple syrup)
- Salt & pepper to taste

Instructions:

1. Slice that red cabbage – aim for thin ribbons that are easy to eat. Chop up the prunes, walnuts, and cilantro. Crumble your cheese and get ready to mix!
2. In a small bowl, whisk together the olive oil, lemon juice, orange juice, honey, salt, and pepper. This is your tangy, citrusy magic potion!
3. Combine the red cabbage, prunes, walnuts, blue cheese, and cilantro in a large bowl. Pour over the citrus dressing and toss gently to coat everything evenly.
4. Grab a fork and enjoy! It's a perfect balance of sweet, salty, tangy, and crunchy.

Warm Couscous Veggie Salad

COOK: 25 MINS I SERVES: 1 I CAL: 350 KCAL

Ingredients

- 1/2 cup uncooked couscous
- 3/4 cup vegetable broth (or water with a bouillon cube)
- 1/2 cup chopped zucchini
- 1/2 cup chopped cucumber
- 1/4 cup crumbled feta cheese (optional, for a vegetarian option omit)
- 1/4 cup chopped sun-dried tomatoes (not packed in oil)
- 2 tbsps chopped fresh parsley
- 1 tbsp each: pumpkin seeds and sunflower seeds
- Pinch of chili flakes (adjust for spiciness)
- 1 tbsp olive oil
- Salt and freshly ground black pepper, to taste

Instructions:

1. Grab your chopping board and get those veggies diced! Toast your seeds if you're feeling fancy (but don't worry, they're delicious either way).
2. Follow the package directions to cook that couscous in your broth. Easy peasy.
3. Heat up some olive oil in a pan and give that zucchini a quick saute. We want it a little softened, not mushy.
4. Throw everything in a bowl – the cooked couscous, the veggies, the seeds, the cheese (if using), and that delish sun-dried tomato action. Don't forget the chili flakes for a bit of spice, and season with salt and pepper to taste. Enjoy!

SOUPS & STEWS

Mediterranean Chickpea & Chicken Soup

COOK: 30 MINS I SERVES: 4 I CAL: 370 KCAL PER SERVING

Ingredients

- 1 tbsp olive oil
- 1 medium onion, chopped
- 1 red bell pepper, chopped
- 2 cloves garlic, minced
- 1 tsp dried oregano
- 4 cups chicken broth

- 1/2 tsp ground cumin
- 1 (15-ounce) can diced tomatoes, undrained (crushed tomatoes work too)
- 1 boneless, skinless chicken breast, cut into bite-sized pieces

- 1 (15-ounce) can chickpeas, rinsed and drained
- 1 cup baby spinach (or other leafy greens)
- Salt and freshly ground black pepper to taste
- Chopped fresh parsley (optional)

Instructions:

1. Grab your chopping board and get those veggies and chicken diced!
2. Get your favorite pot or Dutch oven going on the stovetop over medium heat. Once it's nice and warm, add a drizzle of olive oil. Then, toss in the chopped onion and bell pepper. Let them sizzle and soften up for a few minutes. Finally, add the garlic and cook for another minute, breathing in that amazing aroma that fills your kitchen.
3. Infuse the pan with warmth and fragrance. Add the oregano and cumin, stirring constantly for 30 seconds. Let these aromatics bloom and awaken your senses. Then, pour in the rich chicken broth and vibrant diced tomatoes. Bring the mixture to a lively boil, before lowering the heat and letting it simmer for a gentle 5 minutes.
4. Add the chicken pieces to the simmering broth and cook for 5-7 minutes or until the chicken is cooked. Toss in those rinsed and drained chickpeas and let them warm for about 2 minutes. Now comes the green magic! Add the baby spinach and stir it until just wilted. Give your soup a taste test and season it with salt and pepper to your liking. Garnish with some chopped fresh parsley before serving.

Sunshine Tomato & Lentil Soup

COOK: 30 MINS I SERVES: 4 I CAL: 350 KCAL PER SERVING

Ingredients

- 1 tbsp olive oil
- 1 (28 oz) can crushed tomatoes
- 1 onion, chopped
- 2 cloves garlic, minced
- 4 cups vegetable broth

- 1 cup brown lentils, rinsed
- 1 tsp dried oregano
- 1 small stick of celery
- Salt & pepper to taste
- Fresh parsley, chopped

Instructions:

1. Chop onion & garlic, rinse lentils. Sauté onion in olive oil until softened.
2. Add the minced garlic and cook for another minute, stirring often so it doesn't burn. Pour in those crushed tomatoes and simmer for 1 minute to let the flavors meld.
3. Add broth, lentils, celery, oregano, salt & pepper. Bring to a boil, then simmer for 15-20 minutes or until lentils are tender.
4. Taste & adjust seasonings. Garnish with fresh parsley (optional).

Creamy White Bean & Spinach Soup

Tip: Don't have spinach? You can also use chopped kale or Swiss chard instead. Vegan Vibes? For a vegan approach, try omitting the cheese and adding a touch of your favorite plant-based milk to create a silky smooth sauce.

COOK: 25 MINS | SERVES: 4 | CAL: 250 KCAL PER SERVING

Ingredients

- 1 tbsp olive oil
- 1 onion, chopped
- 2 cloves garlic, minced
- 1 (15 oz) can cannellini beans, rinsed & drained
- 4 cups vegetable broth
- 2 cups packed baby spinach
- 1/2 cup grated Parmesan cheese
- Salt & pepper to taste
- Fresh lemon juice

Instructions:

1. Heat the olive oil in a pot and sauté the chopped onion and garlic until they're softened and fragrant. Think "kissy onions" – that's the goal!
2. After rinsing and draining the cannellini beans, add them to the vegetable broth in the pot. Crank up the heat and bring it to a boil, then let it simmer for a few minutes to let the flavors meld.
3. Throw in that fresh (or frozen) spinach and stir until it wilts. It should only take a minute or two.
4. Now's the time to add that grated Parmesan cheese. Stir it in until it's melted and creamy. Season generously with salt and pepper. For a brighter flavor, consider a squeeze of lemon juice. But it's totally up to you!

Classic Greek Chicken Avgolemono Soup

COOK: 30 MINS | SERVES: 4 | CAL: 300 KCAL PER SERVING

Ingredients

- 1 tbsp olive oil
- 1 onion, chopped
- 2 carrots, chopped
- 4 cups chicken broth
- 2 boneless, skinless chicken breasts
- 2 large eggs, separated
- 1 lemon, juiced
- Salt and freshly ground black pepper
- Fresh dill, chopped

Instructions:

1. Grab your chopping board and dice those veggies! Separate your eggs – yolks in one bowl, whites in another.
2. Heat the olive oil in a large pot over medium heat. Add the onion, carrots, and sauté for a few minutes until softened. Pour in the chicken broth and bring to a simmer. Add the chicken breasts and let them simmer for 10-12 minutes, or until cooked through. Want a vegetarian option? Omit the chicken and use vegetable broth instead. Add more veggies like chopped zucchini or green beans for extra heartiness.
3. Once the chicken is cooked, let the cooked chicken cool slightly, then use two forks to shred it on a clean plate. In a separate bowl, whisk together the egg yolks, lemon juice, and a splash of the hot broth (to temper the yolks). Slowly whisk this mixture back into the simmering broth.
4. Keep whisking constantly over low heat for a few minutes until the soup thickens slightly. Don't let it boil! The egg yolks will cook and curdle if it gets too hot. Season the soup with salt and pepper to taste. Add the shredded chicken back to the pot and warm it. If you used lemon zest, sprinkle it over the soup before serving. Garnish with fresh dill for a pop of color and additional flavor.

Quick & Easy Fish Stew with Mussels

Tip: Don't have fish fillets? You can use shrimp, scallops, or a combination of your favorites. Just adjust the cooking time based on the type of seafood you choose. If you prefer a more brothy stew, add an extra 1/2 cup of white wine (or broth) along with the diced tomatoes.

COOK: 25 MINS I SERVES: 4 I CAL: 300 KCAL PER SERVING

Ingredients

- 1 tbsp olive oil
- 1 onion, chopped (about 1 cup)
- 2 cloves garlic, minced
- 1 (14.5 oz) can diced tomatoes, undrained
- 3/4 pound white fish fillets (cod, haddock or tilapia work well), cut into bite-sized pieces
- 4 cups vegetable broth or fish broth
- 1 pound mussels, scrubbed and debearded
- 1/2 tsp dried oregano
- Salt and freshly ground black pepper, to taste
- Fresh parsley, chopped
- Crusty bread (optional)

Instructions:

1. Chop onion, mince garlic, clean mussels.
2. Awaken the olive oil in your pan with gentle heat. Add the onions and garlic, and sauté them until their fragrance fills the air like a happy song.
3. Pour in those diced tomatoes, broth, oregano, and a pinch of salt and pepper. Let it simmer for a few minutes to let all those flavors get to know each other. Add your bite-sized fish pieces and cook until they're nice and opaque. Add mussels, cover, and cook until open. Garnish, and enjoy with bread.

Moroccan Carrot Chickpea Stew with Lemon

COOK: 25 MINS I SERVES: 4 I CAL: 350 KCAL PER SERVING

Ingredients

- 1 tbsp olive oil
- 1 onion, chopped
- 2 cloves garlic, minced (
- 1 tsp ground ginger
- 1 tsp turmeric
- 1/2 tsp ground cinnamon
- Pinch of saffron (optional)
- 4 cups vegetable broth (low-sodium for a lighter option)
- 1 (15 oz) can chickpeas, rinsed and drained (cannellini beans work too!)
- 1 tbsp chopped preserved lemon (or 1 tsp lemon zest if you don't have preserved lemon)
- 3 carrots, chopped
- Salt and freshly ground black pepper to taste
- Fresh cilantro, chopped

Instructions:

1. Get your olive oil sizzling in a pot over medium heat. Toss in that chopped onion and sauté for about 3 minutes, until it starts to soften. Now add the garlic and all those delicious spices (ginger, turmeric, cinnamon, and maybe even some saffron for extra fancy points). Let them cook for another minute. Pour in your vegetable broth and those rinsed and drained chickpeas. Give it a good stir and let it simmer for a few minutes.
2. Add carrots, simmer 10 minutes (tender-crisp).
3. Stir in preserved lemon (or zest), simmer 2 minutes.
4. Season and serve with cilantro (optional). Like it spicy? Add red pepper flakes with spices.

Spicy Sausage & Kale Stew

Tip: Feeling extra adventurous? To add a touch of warmth and a subtle bite, sprinkle in some red pepper flakes and garlic. Want to add more veggies? Throw in some chopped carrots, bell peppers, or zucchini, along with the onion.

COOK: 25 MINS I SERVES: 4 I CAL: 400 KCAL PER SERVING

Ingredients

- 1 tbsp olive oil
- 1 link spicy Italian sausage, casings removed & crumbled
- 1 onion, chopped (about 1 cup)
- 2 cloves garlic, minced
- 2 carrots, peeled, chopped/sliced
- 2 stalks celery, chopped
- 1 (14.5 oz) can fire-roasted diced tomatoes (undrained)
- 4 cups chicken broth
- 3 cups chopped kale
- Salt & pepper to taste

Instructions:

1. Grab your chopping board and dice that onion and garlic. Crumble your sausage (think tiny meat confetti) and chop your kale. Easy peasy.
2. Heat the olive oil in a pot or Dutch oven and brown that sausage.
3. Toss in the chopped onion, garlic, carrots, and celery. Sauté for 3-4 minutes, or until the vegetables start to soften. Yum!
4. Toss in those fire-roasted tomatoes (with all their juices!) and simmer for a couple of minutes. Let those flavors meld together.
5. Add the chicken broth to the pot and crank up the heat until it reaches a rolling boil. Then, add the chopped kale and simmer for another 5-7 minutes, until it's tender but still has a bit of a bite. Season your stew with salt and pepper to taste. Serve with a Parmesan toast.

Creamy Tomato & Tortellini Soup

COOK: 25 MINS I SERVES: 4 I CAL: 350 KCAL PER SERVING

Ingredients

- 1 tbsp olive oil
- 1 onion, chopped
- 2 cloves garlic, minced
- 1 (28-ounce) can of crushed tomatoes
- 4 cups of chicken or vegetable broth
- 1 cup water
- 1 bay leaf
- 1/2 tsp dried oregano
- Pinch of red pepper flakes
- 1 cup frozen cheese tortellini
- 1/2 cup heavy cream (or milk for a lighter option)
- 1/4 cup grated Parmesan cheese
- Salt and freshly ground black pepper, Fresh parsley, chopped (optional)

Instructions:

1. Gather your ingredients and get chopping! Dice the onion and mince the garlic. Warm the olive oil in a large pot or Dutch oven over medium heat. Once hot, add the chopped onion and cook for 3-4 minutes, stirring occasionally, until softened and translucent. Stir in the minced garlic and cook for an additional minute.
2. Pour in the crushed tomatoes, chicken or vegetable broth, water, bay leaf, oregano, and a pinch of red pepper flakes (if you feel spicy). Bring the mixture to a boil, then reduce heat to low and simmer for 10 minutes.
3. Add the frozen cheese tortellini to the simmering soup. Stir it and cook for an additional 5 minutes or according to package instructions for the tortellini. Once the tortellini are cooked through, stir in the heavy cream (or milk) and grated Parmesan cheese. Season the soup with salt and freshly ground black pepper to taste. Heat through for another minute or two until everything is nice and creamy. Garnish with a sprinkle of fresh parsley.

Veggie Quinoa Power Bowl Soup

COOK: 30 MINS I SERVES: 4 I CAL: 300 KCAL PER SERVING

Ingredients

- 1 tbsp olive oil
- 1 onion, chopped
- 2 cloves garlic, minced
- 1 carrot, peeled and chopped
- 1 celery stalk, chopped
- 1 zucchini, chopped
- 1 (14.5 oz) can diced tomatoes (undrained)
- 4 cups vegetable broth
- 1 cup quinoa, rinsed
- 1 cup chopped baby spinach (or other leafy greens)
- 1/2 cup crumbled feta cheese
- 1/4 cup chopped fresh parsley
- Salt and freshly ground black pepper, to taste

Instructions:

1. Wash and chop all your veggies – onion, garlic, carrots, celery, and zucchini. Rinse the quinoa in a fine-mesh strainer.
2. Heat the olive oil in a large pot or Dutch oven over medium heat. Add the chopped onion and garlic, and sauté for 3-4 minutes, or until the onion is softened and translucent. Add the chopped carrots, celery, and zucchini to the pot. Sauté for another 3-4 minutes or until the vegetables are slightly softened.
3. Add the diced tomatoes, including their flavorful juices, along with the vegetable broth. Stir in the rinsed quinoa, dried oregano, and dried thyme. Season with a generous pinch of salt and pepper.
4. eat the soup to a boil, then simmer on low for 10 minutes or until the quinoa is fluffy and cooked through. Remove the pot from the heat and let it sit for a few minutes to allow the flavors to meld. Taste the soup and adjust the seasonings with additional salt and pepper, if needed. Enjoy!

Lemony Lentil Soup with Orzo

COOK: 25 MINS I SERVES: 4 I CAL: 350 KCAL PER SERVING

Ingredients

- 1 tbsp olive oil
- 1 onion, chopped
- 2 cloves garlic, minced
- 1 carrot, chopped
- 1 celery stalk, chopped
- 1/2 cup orzo pasta
- 1 tsp dried oregano
- 1 tsp dried thyme
- Pinch of red pepper flakes (optional)
- 4 cups vegetable broth
- 1 cup green lentils, rinsed
- 1 (14.5 oz) can diced tomatoes, undrained
- 3/4 cup water
- Juice of 1 lemon
- Salt and freshly ground black pepper
- Fresh parsley, chopped

Instructions:

1. Heat up that olive oil in a pot and toss in the veggies and spices. Let them sizzle and get happy for a few minutes.
2. Add the broth, tomatoes, water, and lentils. Give it a good stir and let it simmer for about 15 minutes or until those lentils are nice and tender.
3. It's time for the orzo to join the party! Stir it in and simmer for another 5 minutes or until it's cooked through.
4. Now for the magic! Squeeze in that lemon juice and season with salt and pepper to taste. Simmer for just one more minute to let all the flavors mingle.
5. Serve & enjoy!

Spanish Chickpea & Vegetable Stew

COOK: 25 MINS I SERVES: 4 I CAL: 320 KCAL PER SERVING

Ingredients

- 2 tbsps olive oil
- 1 onion, chopped
- 2 cloves garlic, minced
- 1 red bell pepper, chopped
- 1 green bell pepper, chopped
- 1 (14.5 oz) can diced tomatoes (undrained)
- 4 cups vegetable broth
- 1 (15 oz) can chickpeas, rinsed and drained
- 1 cup chopped zucchini 1 tsp smoked paprika
- 1/2 tsp dried oregano
- Salt and freshly ground black pepper, to taste
- Fresh parsley, chopped

Instructions:

1. Grab your chopping board and get dicing that onion, garlic, peppers, and zucchini. Rinse those chickpeas and and drain them well. Heat the olive oil and sauté the onion and garlic until they're nice and soft.
2. Add the chopped peppers and cook them for a couple of minutes until they start to soften up.
3. Here comes the fun part! Pour in the diced tomatoes with all their juices and the vegetable broth. Using a spatula, gently scrape up any browned bits from the bottom of the pan – that's where the flavor hides!
4. Now it's party time for the chickpeas, paprika, oregano, salt, and pepper. Give it all a good stir.
5. Bring everything to a boil, then let it simmer for 10 minutes. Once that's done, toss in the zucchini and simmer for another 2-3 minutes. Grab some crusty bread for dipping. If you're feeling fancy, sprinkle on some fresh parsley.

Spicy Shrimp & Tomato Stew

COOK: 25 MINS I SERVES: 4 I CAL: 300 KCAL PER SERVING

Ingredients

- 1 tbsp olive oil
- 1 onion, chopped
- 2 cloves garlic, minced
- 1 red bell pepper, chopped
- 1 (14.5 oz) can fire-roasted diced tomatoes (undrained)
- 1 cup low-sodium chicken broth
- 1 tsp smoked paprika
- 1/2 tsp dried oregano
- Pinch of red pepper flakes (optional)
- 1/2 cup dry white wine (or vegetable broth for a non-alcoholic version)
- 1 pound raw shrimp, peeled and deveined
- 1/4 cup chopped fresh parsley
- Salt and freshly ground black pepper, to taste

Instructions:

1. Grab your chopping board and get dicing that onion, garlic, and bell pepper. Peel those shrimp and get them ready for their fiery bath! Heat some olive oil in a pan and sauté the onion until it's nice and soft. Then, add the garlic and pepper for an extra minute of flavor magic.
2. Throw in those fire-roasted tomatoes (with all their juices!), broth, paprika, oregano, and a pinch of red pepper flakes if you're bold. Let it simmer for a bit to let all the flavors get happy. Are you feeling veggie-licious? Throw in some zucchini, mushrooms, or spinach for extra goodness. If you're using wine, pour it in and let it simmer for a few minutes to cook off the alcohol a bit. Broth works just fine, too!
3. Crank up the heat a little, toss in the shrimp, and cook them until they turn pink and opaque – that's how you know they're done! Stir in the fresh parsley and season everything with salt and pepper to taste.

Tuscan White Bean & Sausage Soup

COOK: 25 MINS I SERVES: 4 I CAL: 350 KCAL PER SERVING

Ingredients

- 1 tbsp olive oil
- 1/2 lb Italian sausage (crumbled)
- 1 onion, chopped
- 2 cloves garlic, minced
- 1 carrot & 1 celery stalk, chopped
- 1 can diced tomatoes (undrained)
- 4 cups chicken broth
- 1 can cannellini beans (rinsed & drained)
- 1/2 tsp dried thyme
- Pinch red pepper flakes (optional)
- Salt & pepper
- Fresh parsley (optional)

Instructions:

1. Chop onion, garlic, carrot, celery. Crumble sausage - no need for fancy techniques; just break it up. Rinse beans.
2. Heat some olive oil in a pot or pan and brown that sausage; drain grease.
3. Toss the chopped onion, garlic, carrot, and celery. Cook them for a few minutes until they're softened up
4. Here comes the fun part - flavor town! Add the diced tomatoes, including their juices, along with the chicken or vegetable broth. Give it a good stir to scrape up any browned bits from the bottom. Bring it to a simmer and let it all hang out for 5 minutes.
5. Add those rinsed cannellini beans and let them simmer for another 5 minutes. They need to get nice and warm. Now's the time to add that thyme and a pinch of red pepper flakes if you're feeling bold. Season everything with salt and pepper to taste - trust your taste buds! Serve! Garnish with parsley (optional). Enjoy with crusty bread.

French Lentil & Vegetable Soup

COOK: 30 MINS I SERVES: 4 I CAL: 300 KCAL PER SERVING

Ingredients

- 1 tbsp olive oil
- 1 onion, chopped
- 2 carrots, peeled and chopped
- 2 celery stalks, chopped
- 2 cloves garlic, minced
- 1 tbsp tomato paste
- 1 cup French green lentils, rinsed and picked over
- 4 cups vegetable broth
- 1 tsp dried thyme
- 1/2 tsp dried rosemary
- Salt and freshly ground black pepper, to taste
- Fresh parsley, chopped (optional)

Instructions:

1. Wash and chop your vegetables - onion, carrots, and celery. Mince the garlic and grab your lentils. Heat the olive oil in a large pot or Dutch oven over medium heat. Add the chopped onion, carrots, and celery. Let the veggies sizzle for a few minutes (for 3-4 minutes) until they're a bit tender. Then throw in the garlic and cook for another minute to wake up the flavors. Finally, stir in that tomato paste to coat everything.
2. Pour in the vegetable broth and add the rinsed French green lentils. Season with dried thyme and rosemary. Give it a good stir and bring to a boil. Reduce heat to low, cover the pot, and simmer for 15-20 minutes or until the lentils are tender. When the lentils are done cooking, stir in salt and freshly ground black pepper to taste.

Greek Meatball Soup

COOK: 25 MINS | SERVES: 4 | CAL: 320 KCAL PER SERVING

Ingredients

For the Meatballs:
- 1/2 pound ground beef
- 1/2 cup uncooked long-grain rice rinsed
- 1/2 cup chopped onion
- 1/4 cup chopped fresh parsley
- 1 tsp olive oil
- 1/2 teaspoon dried oregano
- Salt, freshly ground black pepper

For the Soup:
- 4 cups chicken broth
- 2 tablespoons olive oil
- 1 onion, chopped
- 2 carrots, peeled and chopped
- 2 celery stalks, chopped
- 1 bay leaf
- 1 tsp lemon juice
- 1 cup chopped fresh tomatoes (or 1 (14.5 oz) can diced tomatoes, undrained)
- Salt and freshly ground black

Avgolemono (Egg-Lemon Sauce):
- 2 large eggs
- 1 lemon, juiced (about 2 tablespoons)
- 1/4 cup cold water

Instructions:

1. Grab your chopping board and get those veggies diced. In a bowl, mix up all the meatball ingredients like a champ, then roll them into bite-sized balls. Heat some olive oil in a pot and sauté those veggies Are you feeling veggie-fied? Add some extra chopped veggies to the soup for a more colorful (and healthy!) twist. Add the broth, bay leaf, tomatoes, and lemon juice. Let it simmer for 10 minutes.
2. Toss those meatballs into the simmering soup and cook until they're done.
3. To prevent curdling, temper the eggs. In a separate bowl, whisk together the eggs, lemon juice, and water. Then, slowly drizzle the egg mixture into the simmering soup, whisking constantly (don't let it boil!). This is what makes it nice and creamy! Season the soup with salt and pepper (don't forget!), add some fresh parsley.

Greek Green Bean Fiesta Stew

COOK: 30 MINS | SERVES: 4 | CAL: 300 KCAL PER SERVING

Ingredients

- 1/2 cup olive oil
- 1 large onion, chopped
- 4 cloves garlic, minced
- 4 cups vegetable broth
- 1/2 tsp dried oregano
- 2 medium potatoes, peeled and diced
- 1 (14.5 oz) can diced tomatoes, undrained
- 1 pound fresh green beans, trimmed and cut into bite-sized pieces
- 1/4 cup chopped fresh parsley
- Salt and freshly ground black pepper
- Optional garnishes: crumbled feta cheese, kalamata olives, lemon wedges

Instructions:

1. Wash & chop veggies. Dice the onion, garlic, green beans, and potatoes. Fresh green beans are ideal, but frozen ones won't ruin the dish if you're in a hurry. (thaw and drain first). Heat the olive oil in a large pot or Dutch oven over medium heat. Once hot, add the chopped onion and cook for 3-4 minutes or until softened and translucent. Don't forget to stir occasionally! Toss in the minced garlic and cook for an additional minute. Add the chopped green beans and potatoes to the pot. Mix until coated with olive oil and seasonings.
2. Sauté for 3-4 minutes or until the vegetables start to soften slightly. Add the diced tomatoes, along with their flavorful juices, to the pot. Give it a good stir to scrape up any browned bits from the bottom of the pot. Add the vegetable broth and the dried oregano. Season with a generous pinch of salt and pepper. Increase the heat to bring your stew to a rolling boil. Once bubbling vigorously, reduce the heat to low, cover the pot, and simmer for 15 minutes or until the potatoes and green beans are tender. Stir in the chopped fresh parsley and simmer for an additional minute.

Dreamy Creamy Potato & Kale Soup

COOK: 25 MINS I SERVES: 4 I CAL: 300 KCAL PER SERVING

Ingredients

- 1 tbsp olive oil
- 1 onion, chopped
- 2 cloves garlic, minced
- 1 tsp dried oregano
- 1/2 tsp ground cumin
- 4 cups chopped kale, ribs removed

- Pinch of red pepper flakes (optional, for a bit of heat)
- 4 cups vegetable broth
- 2 pounds potatoes, peeled and diced

- 1/2 cup grated Parmesan cheese (plus extra for garnish, optional)
- Salt and freshly ground black pepper to taste
- Fresh parsley, chopped (optional)

Instructions:

1. Gather your ingredients and get chopping! Dice the onion, garlic, and potatoes. Wash and roughly chop the kale, removing the tough ribs. Heat the olive oil in a large pot or Dutch oven over medium heat. Add the chopped onion and cook for 3-4 minutes or until softened and translucent. Stir in the garlic, oregano, cumin, and red pepper flakes (if using). Let the spices sizzle and release their fragrance for about 30 seconds.
2. Pour in the vegetable broth and heat it to a boil. Add the diced potatoes and season with a generous pinch of salt. Reduce heat to low, cover the pot, and simmer for 15-20 minutes or until the potatoes are tender.
3. Once the potatoes are soft, add the chopped kale and stir it in. Let the kale wilt for 1-2 minutes. Using an immersion blender (or carefully transfer the soup to a blender in batches), blend the soup until it reaches your desired level of creaminess. Aim for a smooth and slightly chunky consistency. Stir in the grated Parmesan cheese and season with additional salt and pepper to taste. Heat through for another minute or two, allowing the cheese to melt and the flavors to come together.

Roasted Tomato Soup

COOK: 30 MINS I SERVES: 4 I CAL: 250 KCAL PER SERVING

Ingredients

- 2 tbsps olive oil
- 4 large ripe tomatoes, sliced
- 1 onion, chopped
- 2 cloves garlic, minced
- 1/2 tsp dried oregano

- 4 cups vegetable broth (low-sodium preferred)
- 1/4 tsp red pepper flakes (optional, for a hint of spice)
- Fresh parsley, chopped (optional)

- 1/2 cup heavy cream (or unsweetened almond milk for a lighter option)
- Salt and freshly ground black pepper to taste

Instructions:

1. Preheat your oven to 400°F (200°C). Toss the sliced tomatoes with 1 tablespoon olive oil on a baking sheet. Season with a pinch of salt and pepper. Roast for 15-20 minutes or until the tomatoes are softened and lightly browned.
2. While the tomatoes roast, heat the remaining 1 tablespoon of olive oil in a large pot or Dutch oven over medium heat. Add the chopped onion and cook for 3-4 minutes or until softened and translucent. Stir in the minced garlic and cook for an additional minute, allowing the garlic to release its fragrance. Once the tomatoes are roasted, carefully transfer them to the pot with the broth mixture. Let the soup cool down a bit. To create a velvety texture, use either an immersion blender in the pot or a regular blender, working in batches.
3. Stir in the heavy cream (or almond milk) and heat through for a minute or two. Season the soup with salt and freshly ground black pepper to taste. Garnish with a sprinkle of chopped fresh parsley (optional).

MAIN COURSES

Creamy Garlic Feta Roasted Veggie Pasta

COOK: 20 MINS I SERVES: 2 I CAL: 280 KCAL PER SERVING

Ingredients

- 1 cup cherry tomatoes
- 1 cup mushrooms
- 1 cup zucchinis
- 1/2 cup asparagus spears
- 1 cup chopped bell pepper
- 8 oz feta cheese
- 1 cup arugula
- 1 tsp dried oregano
- Pinch of salt and pepper
- 8 oz whole-wheat pasta (Spelt pasta works amazing too!)
- 3-4 cloves garlic
- Fresh parsley, chopped
- 2 tbsps of olive oil

Instructions:

1. Gather your ingredients and get chopping! Wash and halve your cherry tomatoes. Slice your mushrooms, zucchinis, and bell pepper.
2. Preheat your oven to 400°F (200°C). Place feta cheese and garlic cloves in the middle of a baking sheet. Spread the chopped veggies around, and toss all ingredients with 2 tbsps of olive oil, oregano, parsley, a pinch of salt, and a sprinkle of pepper. Roast for 20 minutes, or until tender-crisp. While the veggies roast, cook your pasta according to package instructions in a pot of boiling salted water. Once the vegetables and cheese have cooked through, mash the garlic cloves into a paste using a fork. Then, stir the garlicky paste into the feta cheese to create a flavorful sauce.
3. Drain the cooked pasta and add it straight to the creamy feta sauce and veggies. Toss to combine.
4. Divide the pasta, veggies, and creamy sauce between two bowls. Top with arugula. Get ready for a burst of flavor in every bite! It is a symphony of deliciousness, a party in your mouth!

Briam Greek Style Roasted Vegetables

COOK: 30 MINS I SERVES: 2 I CAL: 300 KCAL PER SERVING

Ingredients

- 1 medium eggplant, cut into 1/2-inch cubes
- 1 medium zucchini, cut into 1/2-inch cubes
- 2 small yellow potatoes, cut into 1/2-inch cubes
- 1 red bell pepper, cut into 1/2-inch strips
- 1/2 red onion, thinly sliced
- 1 roma tomato, diced
- 1 clove garlic, minced
- 2 tbsps extra virgin olive oil
- 1/4 cup crumbled feta cheese (optional)
- 1/4 tsp dried oregano
- Salt and freshly ground black pepper, to taste

Instructions:

1. Preheat oven to 400°F (200°C). Lightly grease a baking dish.
2. In a large bowl, combine eggplant, zucchini, potatoes, bell pepper, red onion, diced tomato, garlic, olive oil, oregano, salt, and pepper. Toss to coat. Don't be afraid to substitute! Feel free to use other summer vegetables you have on hand, such as yellow squash, green beans, or cherry tomatoes. To prevent the eggplant from browning too much, sprinkle it with a little salt after cubing and let it sit for 10 minutes. Rinse it well before adding it to the dish.
3. Spread the vegetable mixture evenly in the prepared baking dish.
4. Bake for 20 minutes or until the vegetables are tender and slightly golden brown. Crumble feta cheese over the top and bake for another 2-3 minutes until it's melty and slightly crisp around the edges.

Eggplants & Creamy Garlic Buratta Tomatoes

COOK: 30 MINS I SERVES: 2 I CAL: 360 KCAL PER SERVING

Ingredients

- 2 feisty eggplants
- 300g of red cherry tomatoes
- 1 garlic clove
- Salt and pepper, to taste

- 1 burrata cheese (or 2 if you're feeling extra)
- 30g of finely grated parmesan cheese

- A handful of pine nuts, ready to be toasted
- Fresh parsley or basil for a final flourish
- 2 tbsps olive oil

Instructions:

1. Slice the eggplants lengthwise into 4 proud "fingers." Lavishly coat them with salt and let them rest for 30 minutes. Rinse away the salt and pat them dry with a paper towel. Preheat your oven to 200 degrees. Prepare the garlic clove by simply removing the top. Place it, open-faced, in an oven dish along with the cherry tomatoes. Drizzle them with olive oil, then sprinkle with salt and pepper. Let them roast in the oven for 30 minutes, allowing them to soften and become sweetly caramelized. While the tomatoes get sun-kissed glow, prepare the eggplants for their roasting adventure. Drizzle them with olive oil, then sprinkle with smoky paprika, salt, and pepper. Let them roast for 40 minutes or until they're tender and golden brown. Simply squeeze the roasted garlic cloves out of their skins and mash them into the roasted tomatoes. Keep a few whole tomatoes aside for a pop of color on the final dish.
2. In a separate pan, toast the pine nuts until they become fragrant and a light golden brown. Watch them closely, as they burn very rapidly! Spread the roasted tomato and garlic mixture on a plate. Arrange the roasted eggplant slices artfully on top. Gently tear the burrata cheese and scatter it over the dish. Add the toasted pine nuts and reserved cherry tomatoes for a pop of color. For a burst of freshness, choose either freshly chopped parsley or basil to sprinkle on top, and a dusting of grated parmesan cheese.

Sunshine Pasta with Zesty Herb Sauce

COOK: 25 MINS I SERVES: 2 I CAL: 350 KCAL PER SERVING

Ingredients

- 4 oz (113g) dried pasta (such as penne, farfalle, or rotini)
- 1 tbsp olive oil
- 2 cloves garlic, minced
- 1 shallot, finely minced

- Zest of 1 lemon
- 1/2 cup (packed) fresh basil leaves
- 1/4 cup grated Parmesan cheese
- 1/4 cup walnuts or pine nuts
- 1/4 cup olive oil

- Freshly ground black pepper, to taste
- Salt, to taste
- 1/4 cup reserved pasta water
- Fresh cherry tomatoes or chopped fresh parsley for garnish (optional)

Instructions:

1. In a large pot, bring salted water to a rapid boil. Add your pasta and cook according to the package directions, until it's tender but still firm to the bite (that's al dente!). Reserve about ¼ cup of the pasta water before draining.
2. While the pasta cooks, combine the basil leaves, Parmesan cheese, nuts, olive oil, and a pinch of pepper and salt in a food processor. Pulse until a coarse pesto forms. Grab a knife and chopping board to prep your ingredients. Then, toss them all together in a bowl. Gently warm a film of olive oil in your skillet over medium heat. Add the minced garlic and shallots (if using) and cook until fragrant, about 1 minute. Be careful not to burn the garlic.
3. Add the drained pasta, lemon zest, and pesto to the skillet (or large bowl) with the garlic and shallots (if using). Toss to coat everything evenly. If the mixture seems dry, add the reserved pasta water a tablespoon at a time, until desired consistency is reached. Season with additional salt and pepper to taste. Garnish with fresh cherry tomatoes or chopped fresh parsley (optional) and serve immediately.

Crispy Falafel Bowls with Tahini Sauce

COOK: 30 MINS I SERVES: 2 I CAL: 500 KCAL PER SERVING

Ingredients

Falafel:
- 1 can (15 oz) chickpeas, drained and rinsed
- 1/2 cup chopped red onion
- 1/4 cup chopped fresh parsley
- 1/4 cup chopped fresh cilantro
- 2 cloves garlic, minced
- 2 tbsps all-purpose flour

- 1 ½ tsp ground cumin
- 1 tsp ground coriander
- 1/2 tsp baking powder
- Salt and freshly ground black pepper, to taste

Couscous:
- 1/2 cup couscous
- 3/4 cup boiling water

Vegetables:
- 1 cup chopped cucumber
- 1/2 cup cherry tomatoes, halved
- 1/4 cup crumbled feta cheese (optional)

Tahini Sauce:
- 1/4 cup tahini paste
- 2 tbsps lemon juice
- 2 tbsps water
- 1 clove garlic, minced
- 1-2 tbsps olive oil
- Salt and freshly ground black pepper to taste

Instructions:

1. In a food processor, combine chickpeas, red onion, parsley, cilantro, garlic, flour, cumin, coriander, baking powder, salt, and pepper. Pulse until just combined, taking care not to over-process (the mixture should be slightly coarse).
2. Shape the falafel mixture into small balls, about 1 tablespoon each. Heat a thin layer of olive oil in a skillet over medium heat. Add falafel balls and cook for 3-4 minutes per side or until golden brown and crispy.
3. In a bowl, combine couscous and boiling water. Cover and let sit for 5 minutes or until the couscous is fluffy and translucent. Fluff with a fork. Make the Tahini Sauce: In a small bowl, whisk together tahini paste, lemon juice, water, garlic, olive oil, salt, and pepper until smooth and creamy. Thin with additional water if needed to reach desired consistency. Divide couscous between two bowls. Top with falafel, cucumber, tomatoes, and feta cheese (if using). Drizzle generously with tahini sauce and serve immediately.

Pasta with Winey Broth & Springy Asparagus

COOK: 25 MINS I SERVES: 2 I CAL: 400 KCAL

Ingredients

- 1 tbsp olive oil
- 2 cloves garlic, minced
- 1/4 yellow onion, diced
- 10 asparagus spears, trimmed and cut into 1-inch pieces
- 1/2 cup dry white wine

- 1/4 cup vegetable broth
- 1 tbsp lemon juice
- 1 tbsp chopped fresh parsley
- Salt, freshly ground black pepper
- 4 ounces dried pasta (farfalle, penne, or your favorite variety)
- 1/4 cup grated Parmesan cheese

Instructions:

1. Heat olive oil in a large skillet over medium heat. Add garlic and onion, and cook until softened, about 3 minutes.
2. Add asparagus and cook for an additional 3 minutes or until tender-crisp.
3. Increase heat to medium-high and pour in white wine. Simmer for a quick minute, then gently scrape the pan bottom to incorporate those delicious browned bits. To create a luxuriously thick sauce, whisk in a tablespoon of butter or vegan butter after the white wine has simmered. Stir in vegetable broth, lemon juice, and parsley. Season with salt and pepper to taste. While the sauce simmers, cook pasta according to package directions in a separate pot of boiling salted water. Once cooked, drain the pasta and add it to the skillet with the sauce. Toss to coat evenly.
4. Serve immediately, topped with grated Parmesan cheese (optional). In Italy, we say "Bellissimo"!

Greek Baked Beans in Tomato Sauce

Cannellini beans are a readily available substitute for Gigantes beans in the US. Gigantes beans (elephant beans) are larger and have a slightly nuttier flavor. If you find them, use them. Don't skip rinsing the canned beans! This helps remove excess sodium and gives them a cleaner taste.

COOK: 30 MINS | SERVES: 2 | CAL: 300 KCAL PER SERVING

Ingredients

- 1 can (15 oz) cannellini beans, drained and rinsed (or 1 cup cooked gigantes beans, if available)
- 1 tbsp olive oil
- 1/2 small onion, diced
- 1 clove garlic, minced
- 1 (14.5 oz) can diced tomatoes, undr.
- 1 tbsp tomato paste
- 1/2 tsp dried oregano
- 1/4 tsp ground cinnamon
- 1/4 tsp salt, black pepper
- 1/4 feta cheese (optional)

Instructions:

1. Preheat oven to 400°F (200°C). In a medium oven-safe skillet, heat olive oil over medium heat. Cook the onion until tender and translucent, about 3 minutes. Stir in the garlic and cook for an additional minute, until fragrant.
2. Add the diced tomatoes, tomato paste, oregano, cinnamon, salt, and pepper to the skillet. Stir to combine and bring to a simmer.
3. Add the drained and rinsed cannellini beans to the sauce. Gently stir to coat the beans. Like it spicy? Add a pinch of red pepper flakes for a touch of heat. Like feta cheese ? Add 1/4 cup crumbled feta cheese.
4. Transfer the skillet to the preheated oven and bake for 20 min., uncovered.

Caramelized Onion Pasta

COOK: 30 MINS | SERVES: 2 | CAL: 300 KCAL PER SERVING

Ingredients

- 4 tbsps olive oil
- 2 tbsps unsalted butter
- 2 yellow onions, thinly sliced
- 2 tbsps chili crisp (or substitute with red pepper flakes)
- 1/4 cup chopped fresh parsley
- 500 milliliters of heavy cream
- 1 tsp garlic powder
- Salt and freshly ground black pepper

Instructions:

1. Mix the olive oil and butter in a large skillet over medium heat. Add the sliced onions and cook, stirring occasionally, until softened and caramelized, about 20 minutes. The onions will become golden brown and sweet.
2. Increase the heat slightly and stir in the chili crisp. Let it sizzle for a few seconds, then pour in the heavy cream and garlic powder. Season generously with salt and pepper. Gently heat the sauce until it simmers, then cook for 5 minutes, allowing it to reduce slightly and thicken.
3. Toss the cooked pasta (drained but not rinsed) into the skillet with the sauce. Stir to coat the pasta evenly in the creamy sauce. Let everything simmer for another minute or two, allowing the flavors to meld.
4. Remove the pan from the heat and stir in the chopped parsley. Serve immediately and enjoy this decadent and flavorful pasta dish.

Vegetarian Moussaka

COOK: 30 MINS | SERVES: 2 | CAL: 450 KCAL PER SERVING

Ingredients

- 1 medium eggplant, thinly sliced (about 1/4 inch thick)
- 1/2 tsp salt
- 1 tbsp olive oil
- 1 medium zucchini, thinly sliced
- 1 small potato, thinly sliced

- 1/2 cup chopped onion
- 1 clove garlic, minced
- 1 (14.5 oz) can diced tomatoes, undrained
- 1/2 cup crumbled feta cheese
- 1/4 cup chopped fresh parsley

- 1/4 cup plain Greek yogurt
- 1 tbsp all-purpose flour
- 1/4 cup low-fat milk
- 1/4 teaspoon dried oregano,
- Pinch of freshly ground black pepper

Instructions:

1. Sprinkle the eggplant slices with salt and let them sit for 10 mins. This draws out excess moisture, preventing them from becoming soggy in the dish. Pat the slices dry with paper towels after they've sat. Heat olive oil in a large skillet over medium heat. Add the eggplant slices and cook for 2-3 mins per side or until golden brown. Transfer the cooked eggplant to a plate lined with paper towels to drain excess oil. Repeat this with the zucchini and potato slices, cooking them for about 2 mins per side or until tender-crisp. In the same skillet, add the onion and garlic and cook for 1 min, or until fragrant. Stir in the diced tomatoes and bring to a simmer. Season with salt and pepper to taste. Preheat your oven to 400°F (200°C). In a small bowl, whisk together the Greek yogurt and flour until smooth. Gradually whisk in the milk, oregano, and a pinch of black pepper. In a baking dish (approx. 8x8 inch), spread half of the tomato sauce. Top with half of the browned vegetables, then sprinkle with half of the crumbled feta cheese. Repeat layers with remaining tomato sauce, vegetables, and feta cheese. Pour the yogurt mixture evenly over the top. Bake the moussaka for 20-25 mins or until the top is golden brown and bubbly. Let the moussaka cool for a few minutes before serving, top with fresh parsley.

One-Pan Spiced Chickpea Buddha Bowl

COOK: 30 MINS | SERVES: 2 | CAL: 400 KCAL PER SERVING

Ingredients

- 1 tbsp olive oil
- 1 can (15 oz) chickpeas, drained and rinsed
- 1 tsp ground cumin
- 1/2 tsp smoked paprika
- 1/4 tsp chili powder (adjust for spice preference)

- 1 cup cherry tomatoes, halved
- 1 cup chopped cucumber
- 1 cup crumbled feta cheese (omit for vegan option)
- 1/2 cup chopped fresh parsley
- 1 lemon, cut into wedges
- 2 cups cooked quinoa or brown rice

Optional Add-Ins:
- Kalamata olives, sliced (or any available black olives you have)
- Chopped red onion
- crumbled cooked sausage (for non-vegetarian option)
- crumbled goat cheese
- hummus (drizzled on top)

Instructions:

1. In a large skillet, heat olive oil over medium heat. Tip: If your pan is not oven-safe, transfer the ingredients to a baking dish after sautéing the chickpeas. Add the chickpeas, cumin, paprika, chili powder, salt, and pepper to the pan. Sauté for 5-7 minutes, stirring occasionally, until the chickpeas are golden brown and crispy. Add the cherry tomatoes to the pan and cook for 2-3 minutes, or until they soften and blister. Split the cooked quinoa or brown rice between two bowls. Top with the spiced chickpeas, roasted tomatoes, cucumber, feta cheese (if using), and fresh parsley. Drizzle with a squeeze of lemon juice and serve with additional lemon wedges on the side.

Stuffed bell Peppers with Couscous & Herbs

COOK: 25 MINS I SERVES: 2 I CAL: 400 KCAL PER SERVING

Ingredients

- 2 bell peppers
- 1/2 cup long-grain white rice, rinsed
- 3/4 cup vegetable broth
- 1 tbsp olive oil
- 4 ounces cremini mushrooms
- 1 garlic clove, minced
- 1/4 cup crumbled feta cheese
- 2 tbsps chopped fresh parsley
- 1 tbsp chopped fresh oregano (or 1/2 tsp dried oregano)
- 1/4 tsp salt
- Freshly ground black pepper

Instructions:

1. Preheat oven to 400°F (200°C). Wash the bell peppers and cut off the tops, removing seeds and membranes.
2. In a small saucepan, combine rinsed rice, vegetable broth, and a pinch of salt. Bring to a boil, then reduce heat, cover, and simmer for 15 minutes, or until rice is cooked through and liquid is absorbed. Fluff with a fork and set aside.
3. While the rice cooks, heat olive oil in a skillet over medium heat. Add the sliced mushrooms and cook for 5-7 minutes, or until softened and golden brown. Stir in the minced garlic and cook for an additional minute until fragrant.
4. In a bowl, combine cooked rice, mushrooms, crumbled feta cheese, parsley, oregano, salt, and black pepper. Gently stir to combine. Divide the filling evenly amongst the prepared bell peppers.
5. Place stuffed peppers upright in a baking dish. Roast the peppers until they're soft and yielding and the filling is bubbling hot.

Orzo with Roasted Veggies

COOK: 30 MINS I SERVES: 2 I CAL: 450 KCAL PER SERVING

Ingredients

- 1 red bell pepper, diced
- 1 zucchini, diced
- 1 bunch asparagus, trimmed and cut into 1-inch pieces
- 1 pint cherry tomatoes, halved
- 2 tbsps olive oil
- 1/2 tsp dried oregano
- 1/4 tsp salt, black pepper
- 1 cup orzo pasta
- 4 cloves garlic, minced
- 2 tbsps fresh lemon juice
- 1 tbsp olive oil (for dressing)
- 1/4 cup crumbled feta cheese
- Fresh parsley, chopped

Instructions:

1. Preheat oven to 425°F (220°C). Line a baking sheet with parchment paper. In a large bowl, toss the bell pepper, zucchini, asparagus, cherry tomatoes, olive oil, oregano, salt, and pepper. Distribute the vegetables in a single layer across the surface of the baking sheet. Roast for 20 minutes or until the vegetables are tender-crisp and slightly browned.
2. While the vegetables roast, cook the orzo according to package directions. Drain and set aside.
3. In a small bowl, whisk together the minced garlic, lemon juice, and 1 tablespoon of olive oil. In a large serving bowl, combine the cooked orzo and roasted vegetables. Pour the lemon-garlic dressing over the top and toss to coat.
4. Add crumbled feta cheese and fresh parsley (optional), and serve immediately.

One-Pot Pearl Couscous & Shrimp

COOK: 25 MINS I SERVES: 2 I CAL: 400 KCAL PER SERVING

Ingredients

- 1 tbsp olive oil
- 1/2 small onion, diced
- 2 cloves garlic, minced
- 1 cup pearl couscous
- 1 cup low-sodium chicken broth
- 1/2 tsp dried oregano

- 1 (14.5-ounce) can of diced tomatoes, undrained (fire-roasted recommended for extra flavor)
- 1/4 tsp dried thyme
- 1/4 cup crumbled feta cheese (optional)
- Pinch of red pepper flakes (optional)

- 1/2 pound raw shrimp, peeled and deveined (deveining is optional)
- Salt and freshly ground black pepper, to taste
- Chopped fresh parsley

Instructions:

1. Heat olive oil in a large pot or Dutch oven over medium heat. Add the onion and cook for 3-4 minutes, until softened. Add the garlic and cook for another minute, stirring occasionally until it releases its fragrant aroma.
2. Add the pearl couscous and cook for 1 minute, stirring constantly, to toast the grains slightly.
3. Pour in the diced tomatoes, chicken broth, thyme, oregano and red pepper flakes (if using). Season with salt and pepper to taste. Heat the liquid until boiling, then reduce heat to low, cover the pot, and simmer for 8-10 minutes or until the couscous is cooked through and the liquid is absorbed.
4. While the couscous cooks, season the shrimp with salt and pepper. After 8-10 minutes, stir the shrimp into the pot with the couscous and tomatoes. Cook for 3-4 minutes or until the shrimp are pink and opaque.
5. Remove from heat and stir in feta cheese (if using). Garnish with chopped fresh parsley (if using) and serve immediately.

Pan-Seared Salmon with Lemon & Herbs

COOK: 25 MINS I SERVES: 2 I CAL: 400 KCAL PER SERVING

Ingredients

- 2 (6-ounce) skinless salmon fillets
- 1 tbsp olive oil
- 1/2 tsp dried oregano
- 1/4 tsp garlic powder
- 1/4 tsp dried thyme
- 1 lemon, thinly sliced

- Salt and freshly ground black pepper, to taste
- 2 tbsps chopped fresh parsley (optional)

Instructions:

1. Pat the salmon fillets dry with paper towels. In a small bowl, combine oregano, thyme, garlic powder, salt and pepper. Season the salmon fillets evenly with the spice mixture. Heat up some olive oil in a large skillet over medium-high heat until it starts to shimmer and sizzle. For a richer flavor, use a combination of olive oil and butter to sear the salmon. Carefully place the salmon fillets, flesh-side down, in the hot skillet. Sear for 3-4 minutes or until golden brown and crispy. To check for doneness, gently press the center of the salmon fillet with your finger. If it flakes easily, it's cooked through.
2. Flip and add lemon: Gently flip the salmon fillets and add lemon slices to the pan. Reduce heat to medium and cook for another 3-4 minutes or until the flesh of the salmon separates into flakes when gently pressed with a fork. Transfer the salmon fillets to plates. Spoon the pan juices with the lemon slices over the salmon. Garnish with fresh parsley.

Green Asparagus Risotto with Juicy Shrimp

Tip: No Shrimp? No Problem! This recipe is just as delicious without the shrimp. For a vegetarian twist, you can add other protein options like grilled chicken or tofu.

Leftovers Love You! Risotto tends to stiffen up as it cools. Add a little bit of broth or water to prevent your leftovers from drying out and warm it gently over low heat, stirring frequently, until heated through and creamy again.

COOK: 30 MINS I SERVES: 2 I CAL: 450 KCAL PER SERVING

Ingredients

Risotto Base:
- 1/2 cup Arborio rice
- 4 cups low-sodium chicken broth (or vegetable broth, if you prefer)
- 1 tbsp olive oil
- 1 shallot, finely chopped
- 1/2 cup dry white wine (like Pinot Grigio or Sauvignon Blanc)
- 1 parmesan cheese wedge for grating (about 2 ounces)
- Salt and freshly ground black pepper, to taste

Springtime Stars:
- 8 ounces fresh asparagus, trimmed and cut into bite-sized pieces
- 6 ounces peeled and deveined shrimp (thawed, if frozen)
- 1 tbsp unsalted butter

Instructions:

1. Wash and chop your asparagus into bite-sized pieces. Pat the shrimp dry with paper towels. Grate the Parmesan cheese and have it ready. Finely chop the shallot.
2. In a medium saucepan, heat the chicken or vegetable broth over low heat. Keep it simmering gently – it'll be your secret weapon for creating creamy risotto.
3. Heat the olive oil in a large skillet over medium heat. Then, add the chopped shallot and cook for 2-3 minutes, until softened and fragrant.
4. Add the Arborio rice (or any risotto rice) to the pan and stir it for a minute, letting it toast slightly. This helps develop the rice's nutty flavor.
5. Pour in the white wine and cook, stirring regularly, until the wine thickens and becomes almost undetectable.
6. Here's where the magic happens! Start adding the hot broth, about ½ cup at a time, stirring constantly after each addition. Allow the rice to become creamy and slightly dry before adding another ladle of broth. This slow and steady approach helps create the creamy texture we love in risotto.
7. After about 15 minutes of cooking and adding broth, the rice should be almost cooked through, but still have a slight bite. This is when we add the asparagus! Toss it in and cook for 3-4 minutes or until the asparagus is tender-crisp.
8. In a separate pan, melt the butter over medium heat. Add the shrimp to the skillet and cook, turning occasionally, until they are just cooked through and no longer translucent, about 1-2 minutes per side. Don't overcook them, or they'll become tough and rubbery.
9. Once the asparagus is cooked, stir in the grated Parmesan cheese and a pat of butter (about 1 tablespoon). Season with salt and freshly ground black pepper to taste. Finally, fold in the cooked shrimp. Serve & Savor! Divide the creamy risotto with asparagus and shrimp between two plates and get ready for a taste of spring in every bite!

Tuscan Shrimp Pasta

COOK: 25 MINS I SERVES: 2 I CAL: 350 KCAL PER SERVING

Ingredients

- Large shrimps (10-20, raw and ready for battle)
- 1 pound of your favorite pasta (think penne for pockets of sauce or farfalle)
- 2-3 tbsps of butter (unsalted)
- 2-3 cups of heavy cream
- A generous handful of fresh spinach
- 1-2 containers of cherry tomatoes (10 ounces each), halved
- A sprinkle of garlic powder
- Red pepper flakes (optional)
- 1-1.5 cups of Parmesan cheese (grated, for the perfect finishing touch)
- A dash of Italian seasoning
- Salt and pepper to taste

Instructions:

1. In a separate pan, melt a pat of butter and cook your shrimp until they turn a rosy pink (2-3 minutes), then set them aside for a triumphant return later. In your main pan, melt the remaining butter over medium heat. Summon the heavy cream (2-3 cups) and bring it to a gentle simmer, a creamy potion bubbling forth.
2. While the cream simmers, unleash the pasta: In a pot of boiling water, cook your chosen pasta according to package instructions until it reaches that perfect al dente state. Once your cream simmers, stir in the Italian seasoning, garlic powder, pepper, salt and red pepper flakes (if using). Grate in 1.5 cups of Parmesan cheese, letting it melt into the creamy goodness. Toss the spinach and halved cherry tomatoes into the simmering sauce, letting them mingle for a minute or two.
3. Drain your cooked pasta and add it to the vibrant sauce with your triumphant shrimp. Toss everything together until beautifully coated. Plate your masterpiece and garnish with a final sprinkle of Parmesan cheese.

Garlic Shrimp with Spinach & Tomatoes

COOK: 25 MINS I SERVES: 2 I CAL: 350 KCAL PER SERVING

Ingredients

- 1 tbsp extra virgin olive oil
- 2 cloves garlic, minced
- 1/2 tsp dried oregano
- 1 pint cherry tomatoes, halved
- 5 ounces baby spinach
- Fresh parsley, chopped
- 1 pound large shrimp, peeled and deveined
- 1/4 cup crumbled feta cheese
- Salt and freshly ground black pepper, to taste
- Pinch of red pepper flakes

Instructions:

1. Heat olive oil in a large skillet over medium heat. Add oregano, garlic, and red pepper flakes (if using). Cook for 30 seconds, stirring constantly, until fragrant.
2. Add cherry tomatoes and cook for 2-3 minutes or until they soften and burst.
3. Increase heat to medium-high and add shrimp. Season with salt and pepper. Cook for 2-3 minutes per side until pink and opaque. Don't overcrowd the pan; cook in batches if necessary. Don't overcook the shrimp, they will turn rubbery.
4. Stir in spinach and cook until wilted, about 1 minute.
5. Remove from heat and stir in feta cheese (if using). Serve immediately, garnished with fresh parsley (if using). Serve with a warm, crusty loaf of bread perfect for scooping up every last bit of that incredible sauce!

Tuna Steaks with Nicoise Olive Salad

COOK: 25 MINS | SERVES: 2 | CAL: 450 KCAL PER SERVING

Ingredients

For the Tuna:
- 2 tuna steaks (each about 6 ounces)
- 1 tbsp olive oil
- Salt and freshly ground black pepper, to taste

For the Nicoise Olive Salad:
- 2 cups mixed greens (romaine, arugula, or a blend)
- 1/2 cup cherry tomatoes, halved
- 1/4 cup pitted Kalamata olives, halved (or any available black olives you have)
- 1/2 red onion, thinly sliced
- 2 hard-boiled eggs, quartered
- 2 small red potatoes, boiled, cubed

For the Dressing:
- 2 tbsps olive oil
- 1 tbsp red wine vinegar
- 1/2 tsp Dijon mustard
- 1/4 tsp dried oregano
- Salt, freshly ground black pepper

Instructions:

1. Wash and dry the greens. Halve the cherry tomatoes, pit and halve the Kalamata olives, and thinly slice the red onion. Quarter the hard-boiled eggs and cube the cooked potatoes.
2. Create the flavor base: In a small bowl, whisk together red wine, vinegar, olive oil, Dijon mustard, oregano, salt, and pepper. Set aside.
3. Cook the tuna: Heat olive oil in a large skillet over medium-high heat. Season tuna steaks generously with salt and pepper. Sear the tuna for 2-3 minutes per side for a rare sear or longer for a more cooked steak. For a perfect sear on the tuna, make sure the pan is hot before adding the fish. Don't move the tuna around in the pan while it sears – let it cook undisturbed for a nice crust. To check the doneness of the tuna, gently press the center with your finger. If it's rare, it will be soft and slightly springy. The more cooked it gets, the firmer it will feel.
4. In a large bowl, toss mixed greens, tomatoes, olives, red onion, and cubed potatoes. Drizzle with the prepared dressing and toss to coat. Divide the salad between two plates. Top each salad with a seared tuna steak.

Baked Cod with Puttanesca Sauce

COOK: 30 MINS | SERVES: 2 | CAL: 400 KCAL PER SERVING

Ingredients

- 2 cod fillets (4-6 oz each), skinless and boneless
- 1 tbsp extra virgin olive oil
- 2 cloves garlic, minced
- 1/4 tsp red pepper flakes (adjust to your spice preference)
- 4 anchovy fillets, chopped (optional - omit for a milder flavor)
- 1 (14.5 oz) can diced tomatoes, undrained
- 1/4 cup pitted Kalamata olives, halved (or any other black olives)
- 2 tbsps capers, drained
- 1/4 cup chopped fresh parsley
- Salt and freshly ground black pepper to taste

Instructions:

1. Preheat oven to 400°F (200°C). Lightly grease a baking dish. Dry the cod fillets with paper towels and season with salt and pepper. In a large skillet, heat olive oil over medium heat. Add garlic and red pepper flakes, cook for 30 seconds, until fragrant. (If using anchovies, add them here and cook until dissolved). Stir in diced tomatoes, olives, and capers. Gently simmer for 5 minutes to let the flavors come together.
2. Transfer the sauce to the prepared baking dish. Arrange cod fillets on top of the sauce.
3. Bake the cod (15-20 minutes) until it turns pearly white and breaks apart easily when gently prodded with a fork. Garnish with fresh parsley and serve immediately. Tiny, tender potatoes will be the perfect addition. Enjoy.

Mussels Provençal

COOK: 25 MINS I SERVES: 2 I CAL: 350 KCAL PER SERVING

Ingredients

- 2 pounds fresh mussels, debearded and rinsed
- 1 tbsp olive oil
- 2 cloves garlic, minced
- 1/2 fennel bulb, thinly sliced (optional)

- 1/2 cup dry white wine
- 1 (14.5 oz) can diced tomatoes, undrained
- 1/4 cup chopped fresh parsley
- 1/4 tsp dried thyme
- 1/8 tsp fennel seeds (crushed)

- Pinch of red pepper flakes (optional)
- Salt and freshly ground black pepper to taste
- Crusty bread for serving (optional)

Instructions:

1. In a large pot or Dutch oven, heat olive oil over medium heat. Add garlic and fennel (if using) and cook for 30 seconds until fragrant. Add white wine and scrape the bottom of the pot. Bring to a simmer.
2. Add remaining ingredients: Stir in diced tomatoes, parsley, thyme, fennel seeds (if using), red pepper flakes (if using), salt, and pepper. Bring to a boil.
3. Steam mussels: Add the mussels to the pot and cover immediately. Look for mussels that feel heavy and have tightly closed shells. Choose only mussels with tightly closed shells and not cracked before cooking. Be sure to deveard the mussels by pulling off the beard-like fibers attached to the shell's hinge. You can use a knife or your fingers for this. Cook for 5-7 minutes, shaking the pot occasionally or until the mussels open. Discard any mussels that remain closed.
4. Divide mussels and broth between two bowls. This dish is ready to be devoured! Crusty bread is the perfect partner for soaking up the flavors, but feel free to enjoy it solo.

Greek Baked Cod with Potatoes & Tomatoes

COOK: 30 MINS I SERVES: 2 I CAL: 400 KCAL PER SERVING

Ingredients

- 2 cod fillets (about 6 oz each)
- 1 pound russet potatoes, peeled and cut into 1-inch cubes
- 1 cup cherry tomatoes
- 1/2 red onion, thinly sliced
- 2 tbsps olive oil

- 1/4 cup crumbled feta cheese
- 1 tbsp chopped fresh oregano
- 1/2 lemon, juiced
- 1/4 tsp dried thyme
- Salt and freshly ground black pepper to taste

Instructions:

1. Preheat oven to 400°F (200°C). Lightly grease a baking dish.
2. In a large bowl, toss potatoes with thyme, oregano, olive oil, salt, and pepper. Spread potatoes evenly in the prepared baking dish. Place the cod fillets over the potatoes. Scatter cherry tomatoes and red onion slices around the cod. Don't overcrowd the pan! If your baking dish is too small, use two separate dishes to ensure even cooking.
3. Drizzle the fish and vegetables with lemon juice. Season with additional salt and pepper, if desired.
4. Bake until the cod is cooked through (opaque and flakes easily with a fork) and the potatoes are tender, about 20-25 minutes. (Optional) For a salty, creamy finish, top with crumbled feta cheese during the last 2 minutes of baking.
6. Garnish with fresh herbs like parsley or dill (optional) and serve immediately.

Spicy Mussels in Tomato Broth

COOK: 25 MINS I SERVES: 2 I CAL: 350 KCAL PER SERVING

Ingredients

- 1 small yellow onion, finely chopped (about 1/2 cup)
- 2 cloves garlic, minced
- 1 (14.5-ounce) can diced tomatoes, undrained
- 1/2 tsp dried oregano
- 1 tbsp olive oil
- 1/4 tsp red pepper flakes (adjust to your spice preference)
- 1/4 cup dry white wine (optional)
- 1/4 cup chopped fresh parsley
- 1 pound fresh mussels, debearded and scrubbed
- Salt and freshly ground black pepper,
- Crusty bread, for serving (optional)

Instructions:

1. Debeard and scrub the mussels. Finely chop the onion and garlic. Chop the fresh parsley. Heat olive oil in a large pot or Dutch oven over medium heat. Add the onion to your pan and cook it over medium heat, stirring occasionally, until it becomes soft and translucent. This will take about 3 minutes. Then, add the garlic and cook for another minute until you can smell its fragrant aroma. Stir in the diced tomatoes, oregano, and red pepper flakes. Simmer for 5 minutes, starting from a boil. If using white wine, add it now and simmer for an additional 2 minutes.
2. Look for mussels that feel heavy for their size and have tightly closed shells. Discard any mussels that don't have sealed entirely shells. Debearding mussels simply means pulling off the beard, a fibrous strand attached to the shell's hinge. You can use your fingers or a pair of pliers, which might be helpful here.
3. Steam Mussels: Add the mussels to the pot, increase heat to medium-high, and cover tightly. Steam for 5-7 minutes, shaking the pot occasionally, or until the mussels open. Discard any mussels that remain unopened.
4. Remove the pot from heat and stir in the chopped parsley. Season with salt and pepper to taste. Divide the mussels and broth between two serving bowls and serve immediately with crusty bread for dipping, if desired.

Spanish Mussels with Chorizo

COOK: 30 MINS I SERVES: 2 I CAL: 350 KCAL PER SERVING

Ingredients

- 1 pound mussels, debearded and rinsed
- 1 tsp olive oil
- 2 ounces cured Spanish chorizo, diced (about ½ cup)
- 1/4 tsp dried thyme
- 1 shallot, finely chopped
- 2 garlic cloves, minced
- 1/2 cup dry white wine (such as Pinot Grigio or Sauvignon Blanc)
- 1 (14.5-ounce) can diced tomatoes, undrained
- Pinch of red pepper flakes (optional)
- Freshly ground black pepper
- Chopped fresh parsley for garnish (optional)
- Crusty bread for serving

Instructions:

1. Debeard and rinse the mussels. Mussels often have beard-like strands attached to their shells. To remove, firmly grasp a beard and pull it down towards the pointed end of the mussel, discarding the beard.
2. Finely chop the shallot and garlic. Heat olive oil in a large pot or Dutch oven over medium heat. Add the chorizo to the pan and cook, stirring occasionally, until it browns and crisps on the edges. The fat should also cook out during this time. Add shallot and garlic, cook until softened, about 1 minute more. Pour in white wine and scrape up any browned bits from the bottom of the pot. Add diced tomatoes, thyme, and red pepper flakes (if using). Bring to a simmer. Add mussels to the pot, nestling them in the broth. Steam the mussels for 5-7 minutes or until they've all opened wide. Discard any mussels that remain unopened. Season with black pepper to taste. Divide mussels and broth among two bowls. Garnish with fresh parsley (optional) and serve with crusty bread for dipping in the delicious broth.

Seared Scallops with Lemon Risotto

COOK: 30 MINS I SERVES: 2 I CAL: 500 KCAL PER SERVING

Ingredients

For the Scallops:
- 8 large sea scallops (U10-U12 size), side muscle removed
- 1 tbsp olive oil, 2 tbsps unsalted butter
- 1/2 lemon, juiced (about 2 tsps)
- Salt and freshly ground black pepper

For the Lemon Risotto:
- 1 tbsp olive oil
- 1/2 small yellow onion, diced
- 1 clove garlic, minced
- 1 cup Arborio rice
- 2 tbsps unsalted butter

- 1/2 cup dry white wine (such as Pinot Grigio)
- 4 cups low-sodium chicken broth, warm
- 1/4 cup grated Parmesan cheese
- 1 lemon, zested (about 1 tsp)
- Salt & freshly ground black pepper taste

Instructions:

1. Dry the scallops completely using paper towels. Season them generously with salt and pepper. Cook the risotto: Heat olive oil (medium heat) in a large saucepan. Add onions and cook until softened (3 minutes). Stir in the garlic and cook for an additional minute until fragrant. Add the Arborio rice (or any type of risotto rice) and cook, constantly stirring, until the rice becomes translucent, about 1 minute. Pour in the white wine and cook, stirring occasionally, until the wine is absorbed. Slowly pour in the warmed chicken broth, about 1/2 cup at a time. Stir the rice constantly, allowing it to absorb the delicious broth before adding another portion. Continue this process for about 15-20 mins or until the rice is tender but still has a slight bite in the center.
2. While the risotto cooks, sear the scallops. Heat another tablespoon of olive oil and 1 tablespoon of butter in a large skillet over medium-high heat. Once the oil shimmers, add the scallops to the hot pan and cook undisturbed for 2-3 mins or until golden brown and opaque on the bottom. Flip the scallops and cook for an additional 1-2 mins or until just cooked through. Once the risotto is cooked, stir in the Parmesan cheese, remaining 1 tbsp of butter and lemon zest. Season with salt and pepper to taste. Divide the risotto between two plates and top each with the seared scallops. Drizzle with any pan drippings from the scallops and serve immediately.

Mediterranean Fish Tacos

COOK: 25 MINS I SERVES: 2 I CAL: 400 KCAL PER SERVING

Ingredients

- 1 pound skinless, boneless white fish fillets (cod, tilapia, halibut, or mahi-mahi all work well)
- 1 tbsp olive oil
- 1 tsp dried oregano

- 1/2 tsp ground cumin
- Salt and freshly ground black pepper, to taste
- 1/4 tsp garlic powder
- 4 small corn tortillas
- 1/2 cup crumbled feta cheese

- 1/4 cup chopped red onion
- 1 roma tomato, diced
- 1/4 cup chopped fresh parsley
- 2 tbsps plain Greek yogurt
- 1 tsp lemon juice
- 1/4 tsp dried dill weed

Instructions:

1. Pat the fish dry with paper towels. Cut the fish into bite-sized pieces. In a small bowl, combine olive oil, garlic powder, cumin, oregano, salt, and pepper. For a smoky flavor, sprinkle the fish with smoked paprika and other spices. Heat a large skillet over medium heat. Add the fish and cook for 3-4 minutes per side or until cooked through and flaky. While the fish cooks, give your tortillas a quick sear! Use a dry skillet on medium heat. Heat each tortilla for 30 seconds a side to get them nice and warm, or wrap them in a damp paper towel and microwave for 30 seconds. Make these tacos gluten-free by using corn tortillas. In a small bowl, whisk together lemon juice, Greek yogurt, dill weed, and a pinch of salt and pepper. Assemble the Tacos: Spread a dollop of sauce on each warmed tortilla. Top with cooked fish, crumbled feta cheese, red onion, diced tomato, and fresh parsley. Enjoy!

Mediterranean Tuna Burgers

COOK: 25 MINS | SERVES: 2 | CAL: 400 KCAL PER SERVING

Ingredients

- 1 (5 oz) can chunk light tuna in water, drained
- 1/2 cup chopped red onion
- 1/4 cup crumbled feta cheese
- 1/4 cup chopped fresh parsley
- 1 tbsp mayonnaise
- 1 tbsp chopped fresh dill (or 1/2 tsp dried dill)
- 1 tablespoon lemon juice
- 1 clove garlic, minced
- 1/4 cup panko bread crumbs
- 1/4 tsp dried oregano
- Salt and freshly ground black pepper to taste
- 2 hamburger buns, toasted (optional)
- crumbled feta cheese and chopped fresh parsley for garnish (optional)

Instructions:

1. In a large bowl, combine flaked tuna, red onion, feta cheese, parsley, dill, mayonnaise, lemon juice, garlic, oregano, salt, and pepper. For a richer flavor, use canned tuna packed in olive oil. Drain the oil well before using. Don't over-mix the tuna mixture. A light hand will help prevent dry burgers.
2. Gently fold in the panko breadcrumbs until just combined. If the mixture seems too wet, add a little more panko breadcrumbs. Separate the mixture into two halves and shape each half into a patty.
3. Heat a lightly oiled skillet over medium heat. Cook the burgers for 4-5 minutes per side or until golden brown and cooked through. You can cook these burgers on a grill pan, outdoor grill, or in a skillet.
4. Serve burgers on toasted buns (if using) and top with a vibrant confetti of crumbled feta and chopped parsley.

Seared Scallops with Creamy Tomato Pasta

COOK: 25 MINS | SERVES: 2 | CAL: 500 KCAL PER SERVING

Ingredients

- 1 tbsp olive oil
- 2 shallots, finely minced
- 2 cloves garlic, minced
- 1 (14.5 oz) can diced tomatoes, undrained
- 1 tsp dried oregano
- 1/2 tsp dried basil
- 1/4 tsp red pepper flakes (optional)
- Salt and freshly ground black pepper
- 1/2 cup heavy cream
- 4 ounces pasta (linguine, fettuccine, or angel hair work well)
- 8 sea scallops (dry sea scallops are best for searing)
- Fresh parsley, chopped, for garnish

Instructions:

1. In a small bowl, whisk together the heavy cream, oregano, basil, red pepper flakes (if using), and a pinch of salt and pepper. Set aside. Bring a pot of salted water to a boil. Add the pasta and cook according to package directions until al dente (usually about 8-10 minutes). Don't drain all the water! Grab ½ cup with a measuring cup before straining. While the pasta cooks, heat olive oil in a large skillet over medium heat. Sauté the chopped shallots and garlic for roughly 2 minutes or until they become tender. Stir in the diced tomatoes with their juices, scraping up any browned bits from the bottom of the pan. Bring to a simmer and cook for 5 minutes, until slightly thickened.
2. Heat another large skillet over high heat. Season the scallops with salt and pepper. Add the scallops to the hot pan and sear for 1-2 minutes per side or until golden brown and cooked through. Be careful not to overcrowd the pan, and cook the scallops in batches if necessary. Reduce the heat of the tomato sauce pan to low. Pour in the cream mixture and stir to combine. Add the cooked and reserved pasta water (a little at a time) until the sauce reaches the desired consistency. Season with additional salt and pepper to taste. Prepare two plates with equal portions of pasta and sauce. Top each plate with seared scallops and garnish with fresh parsley, if desired.

Salmon with Lemony Feta Rice

COOK: 25 MINS I SERVES: 2 I CAL: KCAL PER SERVING

Ingredients

For the Salmon:
- 1 lb salmon fillets
- 1/2 tsp smoked paprika
- 1/4 tsp dried oregano
- 1/4 tsp dried parsley
- Pinch of red chili flakes
- 1.5 tbsp olive oil, divided
- Pinch of salt

For the Lemony Feta Rice:
- 3/4 cup cooked jasmine rice
- 1 can (7.5 oz) chickpeas, drained and rinsed
- 3 oz cherry tomatoes (mixed colors), halved
- 1/4 cup kalamata olives, sliced (or other black olives)
- 1/4 cup green olives, sliced
- 1.5 tbsp freshly squeezed lemon juice

For the Feta Topping:
- 3 oz feta cheese, crumbled
- 1/2 tbsp olive oil
- 1/2 tbsp freshly squeezed lemon juice
- Pinch of dried oregano (more to taste)
- 1 tbsp fresh oregano, chopped (opt.)
- Fresh oregano sprigs, for garnish (optional)

Instructions:

1. Sizzle the Salmon: Heat a large skillet (cast iron works great!) over medium heat for 4 minutes. Season the salmon with smoked paprika, oregano, parsley, chili flakes, and salt. Drizzle the seasoned fish with 1 tablespoon olive oil. Once the pan is hot, add the other 2 tablespoons of olive oil. Carefully place the salmon fillets, skin-side up, in the skillet. Cook undisturbed for 4 minutes on medium-high heat. Flip the salmon carefully and cook 5 more minutes on medium heat. Remove the cooked salmon to a plate. Using a spatula, carefully separate the flesh from the skin. Discard the skin or save it for a crispy snack. Wipe the skillet clean with paper towels.
2. Add the cooked rice, chickpeas, tomatoes, and olives to the empty skillet. Pour in the lemon juice and reheat on medium heat, stirring everything together. For additional flavor, drizzle with an extra tablespoon of olive oil. Season with salt and pepper to taste.
3. Creamy Feta Delight: In a bowl, combine crumbled feta cheese, olive oil, lemon juice, dried oregano, and fresh oregano (if using). Mix well to coat the feta with the flavorful herb and oil mixture.
4. Add half of the feta cheese mixture to the skillet with the rice and stir gently to combine. Place the cooked salmon back into the skillet and reheat on medium heat. Top the dish with the remaining feta mixture and a sprinkle of fresh oregano sprigs for a touch of elegance (optional). Serve immediately and dive into the vibrant flavors of the Mediterranean!

Fiery Fiesta Squid with Garlic & Herb Drizzle

COOK: 20 MINS I SERVES: 2 I CAL: 420 KCAL PER SERVING

Ingredients

- A squadron of fresh squid tubes (around 8)
- Extra virgin olive oil, enough for a drizzle and a sizzle (around 6-8 tbsps)
- Sea salt, to season
- 6 valiant cloves of garlic, chopped
- 1 fiery red chili, diced (remove the seeds for a milder dish)
- A generous handful of parsley, chopped
- Lemon juice, a squeeze to brighten things up (about 1/4 of a lemon)

Instructions:

1. Prep the squid: score, pat the squid squad dry with a paper towel, and set aside. Heat oil in a pan scorching hot. Sear squid for 2 minutes per side, season with salt, and remove. Add more oil reduce heat.
2. Throw in the garlic, chili, and parsley. Sauté the mix for a minute or so, until the garlic turns a golden brown – that's when they've released their fragrant magic. Reunite the squid, toss for 30 seconds, and add a squeeze of lemon juice. Serve squid drizzled with flavorful oil. Enjoy your victory!

Lemon Garlic Chicken with Roasted Vegetables

COOK: 30 MINS I SERVES: 2 I CAL: 400 KCAL PER SERVING

Ingredients

- 2 bone-in, skin-on chicken thighs (or boneless, skinless breasts)
- 1 tbsp olive oil
- 1 lemon, juiced (about 2 tbsps)
- 1 tsp dried oregano
- 1/2 tsp garlic powder
- 1/4 tsp salt
- 1/4 tsp black pepper
- 1 medium red bell pepper (chunks)
- 1 medium zucchini (chunks)
- 1/2 red onion, cut into wedges
- 1 cup cherry tomatoes

Instructions:

1. Preheat oven to 400°F (200°C). Lightly grease a rimmed baking sheet.
2. In a small bowl, whisk together lemon juice, olive oil, garlic powder, oregano, salt, and pepper.
3. Place chicken in a bowl and toss with half of the marinade. For added flavor, marinate the chicken for 15-20 minutes in the lemon juice and herb mixture before roasting.
4. In a separate bowl, toss vegetables with the remaining marinade. Asparagus, broccoli florets, or Brussels sprouts would all be delicious additions. Arrange the vegetables in a single layer on the baking sheet. Scatter the chicken pieces evenly over the bed of vegetables. Roast for 20-25 minutes, or until chicken is cooked and vegetables are tender-crisp. Bone-in, skin-on chicken thighs will take longer to cook through than boneless, skinless breasts. Adjust cooking time accordingly, or use a meat thermometer to ensure the internal temperature reaches 165°F (74°C). The chicken juices should run clear when pierced with a fork.

Moroccan Chicken with Couscous

COOK: 30 MINS I SERVES: 2 I CAL: 450 KCAL PER SERVING

Ingredients

- 1 tbsp olive oil
- 1 pound boneless, skinless chicken breasts, cut into bite-sized pieces
- 1/2 tsp ground cumin
- 1/4 tsp ground coriander
- 1/4 tsp ground ginger
- 1/4 tsp turmeric
- Pinch of cinnamon
- Salt and freshly ground black pepper, to taste
- 1 medium red onion, chopped
- 1 medium carrot, diced
- 1 cup low-sodium chicken broth
- 1 cup instant couscous
- 1/2 cup dried golden raisins
- 1/4 cup chopped fresh parsley
- Sliced almonds (optional, for garnish)

Instructions:

1. Heat olive oil in a large skillet over medium heat. Season chicken with cumin, coriander, ginger, turmeric, cinnamon, salt, and pepper. For added flavor, marinate the chicken in the spices and a tablespoon of olive oil for 15 minutes before cooking. Sear the chicken in the hot pan for 5-7 minutes, until it's nicely browned on all sides and cooked through.
2. Add the chopped carrot and onion to the pan with the chicken. Cook for 5 minutes, or until the vegetables are softened. Stir in the chicken broth and dried raisins. Bring to a boil, then reduce heat to low. Cover and simmer for 5 minutes.
3. Stir in the couscous and remove the pan from the heat. Fluff the couscous with a fork and let it sit for 5 minutes, covered, to absorb the remaining liquid. Finish with a sprinkle of vibrant parsley and slivered almonds for an extra touch of flavor and texture.

Yogurt Chicken Souvlaki & Honey Feta Carrots

COOK: 30 MINS I SERVES: 2 I CAL: 550 KCAL PER SERVING

Ingredients

Chicken Souvlaki
- 1 boneless, skinless chicken breast (about 1/2 lb)
- 1/2 cup plain Greek yogurt
- 2 tbsps olive oil
- 1 tbsp lemon juice
- 1 tsp dried oregano
- 1/2 tsp garlic powder
- 1/2 tsp dried thyme
- 1/4 tsp salt, pinch of black pepper
- 1 red bell pepper, cut into chunks
- 1 red onion, cut into wedges
- 8 wooden skewers (soaked in water for 10 min, optional)

- **Honey Feta Carrots**
- 1 pound carrots, peeled and cut into batons (batons are similar to thick sticks)
- 1 tbsp olive oil, 1 tbsp honey
- 1 clove garlic, minced
- 1/2 tsp dried dill (or 1 tbsp fresh dill, chopped)
- 1/4 tsp salt
- 1/4 cup crumbled feta cheese
- Cracked black pepper, to taste (optional)

Instructions:

1. **Chicken Souvlaki:** Cut the chicken breast into 1-inch cubes. In a medium bowl, whisk together olive oil, lemon juice, the Greek yogurt, oregano, garlic powder, thyme, salt, and pepper. Add the chicken and toss to coat. Thread the chicken cubes, red bell pepper chunks, and red onion wedges onto the soaked wooden skewers (if using). Make sure the ingredients are evenly spaced for proper cooking. Get your grill pan (or grill) hot over medium heat. Cook the skewers on the grill until the chicken is juicy and cooked through and the vegetables are tender but still have a bit of a bite. **Honey Feta Carrots**: Preheat your oven to 425°F (220°C) and line a baking sheet with parchment paper. In a large bowl, toss the carrots with olive oil, honey, garlic, dill, and salt. Make sure the carrots are evenly coated. Spread the carrots out on the prepared baking sheet in a single layer. Roast for 20-25 minutes or until the carrots are tender-crisp, and slightly caramelized around the edges. Remove from the oven and sprinkle with feta cheese. Grind some fresh black pepper over the top for an extra flavor boost. Enjoy!

Honey Dijon Chicken with Goat Cheese

COOK: 25 MINS I SERVES: 2 I CAL: 400 KCAL PER SERVING

Ingredients

- 2 boneless, skinless chicken breasts (around 5-6 oz each)
- 2 tbsps Dijon mustard
- 1 tbsp honey
- 1 tbsp olive oil
- 1/4 cup low-fat plain yogurt
- 1/4 cup crumbled goat cheese
- 1/4 tsp dried oregano
- Salt and freshly ground black pepper to taste
- 2 tbsps chopped fresh parsley (optional, for garnish)
- Arugula leaves, pine nuts (opt.)

Instructions:

1. Preheat oven to 400°F (200°C). Lightly grease a baking dish. Pat chicken breasts dry with paper towels. Season the breasts on both sides with salt and pepper. In a small bowl, whisk together olive oil, Dijon mustard, honey, yogurt, oregano, salt, and pepper. For thicker sauce, use full-fat Greek yogurt instead of low-fat plain yogurt. Want a bit more spice? Add a pinch of red pepper flakes to the sauce mixture. Place chicken breasts in the prepared baking dish. Spread half the Dijon sauce over each chicken breast.For perfectly cooked chicken, bake for 15-20 minutes and aim for an internal temperature of 165°F (74°C). Remove the chicken from the oven and top each breast with half the goat cheese. Broil for 1-2 minutes or until goat cheese is melted and slightly golden brown. Garnish with fresh parsley (optional) and serve immediately with remaining Dijon sauce on the side for dipping. Pair this dish with peppery arugula leaves and toasted pine nuts for a delightful contrast.

Italian Chicken Piccata & Lemon Caper Sauce

COOK: 30 MINS I SERVES: 2 I CAL: 400 KCAL PER SERVING

Ingredients

- 1 tbsps unsalted butter
- 1/4 cup dry white wine (such as Pinot Grigio or Sauvignon Blanc)
- 2 boneless, skinless chicken breasts (thinly pounded to about 1/2-inch thickness)
- 1/4 cup all-purpose flour
- 1/2 cup chicken broth
- Juice and zest of 1 lemon
- 2 tbsps drained capers
- Fresh parsley (chopped, for garnish - optional)
- 1/2 tsp salt, 1/4 tsp freshly ground black pepper

Instructions:

1. Prepare all ingredients. Pound the chicken breasts to an even thickness. In a shallow bowl, whisk together the flour, salt, and pepper. In a separate plate, beat the egg. Evenly coat each chicken breast in the seasoned flour mixture. Ensure thorough coverage by dipping it completely in the beaten egg. Heat some olive oil in a large pan over medium. Sear the chicken breasts for 3-4 minutes a side (flip once for even cooking) until golden brown and cooked through. Remove the chicken from the pan and set aside. Add the butter to the same skillet over medium heat. Once melted, whisk in the white wine, but chicken broth can be substituted if preferred, scraping up any browned bits from the bottom of the pan. Bring the wine to a low simmer for 1 minute, then add the chicken broth, lemon zest and lemon juice. Increase heat until boiling, then reduce and simmer for 2-3 minutes, or until the sauce thickens slightly. Stir in the capers and return the chicken to the pan. Spoon the sauce over the chicken and cook for an additional minute to heat through. Serve immediately with your favorite sides, such as pasta, rice, or roasted vegetables. Garnish with fresh parsley, if desired.

Lemony Chicken & Orzo in a Creamy Dream

COOK: 30 MINS I SERVES: 2 I CAL: 400 KCAL PER SERVING

Ingredients

- 1 boneless, skinless chicken breast (around 6 oz)
- 1/2 cup orzo
- 1 tbsp olive oil
- 1/2 onion, diced, 1 clove garlic
- 1/2 cup chicken broth
- 1/2 cup heavy cream
- 1/4 cup grated Parmesan cheese
- 1 lemon: juiced (around 2 tbsps) and zested (1 tsp)
- 1/4 tsp dried thyme
- Salt and freshly ground black pepper, to taste
- Fresh parsley, chopped (for garnish, optional)

Instructions:

1. Slice the chicken breast into thin strips. Season with salt and pepper. Cook the orzo: Heat a large pan with olive oil over medium heat (just until it shimmers!). Add the orzo and cook, stirring occasionally. Watch for the orzo to develop a nutty aroma and a slightly toothsome texture for about 2 minutes. Sauté the diced onion until it softens, roughly 3 minutes. Stir in the minced garlic and cook for another minute until fragrant. Simmer the orzo: Pour in the chicken broth, lemon juice, and thyme. Bring to a simmer, then stir in the orzo. Reduce heat to low, cover, and simmer for 8-10 minutes until the orzo is tender and most of the liquid is absorbed. Once the orzo is cooked, stir in the heavy cream (or milk) and Parmesan cheese. Let it simmer for another minute or two until the sauce thickens slightly. In with the chicken: Add the chicken strips to the pan and cook for 3-4 minutes, or until cooked through and golden brown.
Season with additional salt and pepper to taste. Remove from heat and stir in the lemon zest. Plate the creamy orzo and chicken, garnished with fresh chopped parsley (optional).

Harissa Chicken & Roasted Sweet Potatoes

COOK: 25 MINS I SERVES: 2 I CAL: 450 KCAL PER SERVING

Ingredients

- 1/4 tsp salt
- 1/4 tsp black pepper
- 1 pound boneless, skinless chicken thighs (or breasts, cut into bite-sized pieces) medium sweet potato, peeled and cut into 1-inch cubes

- 1/2 red onion, thinly sliced
- 1 tbsp olive oil
- 2 cloves garlic, minced
- 2 tbsps harissa paste
- 1 tsp honey
- 1/2 lemon, juiced (about 1 tbsp)
- 1/2 tsp dried oregano

Instructions:

1. Preheat oven to 400°F (200°C). Lightly grease a rimmed baking sheet.
2. In a large bowl, whisk together olive oil, garlic, harissa paste, honey, lemon juice, oregano, salt, and pepper. * Prefer a milder dish? Reduce the harissa paste to 1 tbsp or choose a lighter paste variety.
3. Add chicken pieces to the bowl and toss to coat evenly.
4. Stir in sweet potato cubes and red onion slices. Want to add more veggies? Toss in chopped broccoli florets or sliced bell peppers with the sweet potatoes.
5. Scatter the chicken and vegetables on the prepared baking sheet, making sure none of them overlap. Don't overcrowd the pan! If your pan seems small, roast the chicken and veggies in batches to ensure even cooking.
6. Pop it in the oven for 20-25 minutes, or until the chicken is golden brown and the veggies are delightfully softened, giving everything a good flip halfway through.

Chicken with Sun-Dried Tomatoes & Spinach

COOK: 25 MINS I SERVES: 2 I CAL: 400 KCAL PER SERVING

Ingredients

- 1 tbsp olive oil
- 2 boneless, skinless chicken breasts (around 1/2 lb each)
- 1/2 tsp dried oregano
- 1/4 tsp garlic powder
- Salt and freshly ground black pepper, to taste

- 1/2 cup chopped onion
- 3 cloves garlic, minced
- 1/2 cup chopped sun-dried tomatoes (not packed in oil)
- 1 cup fresh baby spinach
- 1/4 cup crumbled feta cheese (opt.)
- 2 tbsps chopped fresh parsley (opt.)

Instructions:

1. Wash and pat chicken breasts dry with paper towels. Season them generously with oregano, garlic powder, salt, and pepper. Chop the onion, garlic, and sun-dried tomatoes. Rinse the spinach. Heat olive oil in a large skillet over medium-high heat. Slide the chicken breasts into the pan and let them cook for 5-7 minutes on each side. You can take them out when they're nice and golden brown, and cooked all through. Once golden brown, move the chicken to a plate. Lower heat to medium and add onion to the pan. Cook for 2-3 minutes or until softened. Add the garlic and cook for another minute, until fragrant. Add sun-dried tomatoes and cook for 1 minute more. Add spinach and cook, stirring often, till wilted. Season with salt & pepper if needed. Return the cooked chicken breasts to the pan and spoon the spinach mixture over them. Garnish with crumbled feta cheese and fresh parsley (optional). Enjoy hot with roasted veggies or brown rice.

Tuscan Chicken with White Beans

COOK: 30 MINS I SERVES: 2 I CAL: 400 KCAL PER SERVING

Ingredients

- 1 tbsp extra virgin olive oil
- 2 boneless, skinless chicken breasts (about 6 oz each)
- 1/2 tsp dried oregano
- 1/4 tsp garlic powder
- 1/4 tsp salt
- 1/4 tsp black pepper
- 1/2 medium onion, diced
- 2 cloves garlic, minced
- 1 (14.5 oz) can diced tomatoes, undrained
- 1 (15 oz) can cannellini beans, drained and rinsed
- 1/4 cup chopped fresh parsley (opt.)

Instructions:

1. Heat olive oil over medium heat in a large skillet. Season the chicken breasts with oregano, garlic powder, salt, and pepper. For maximum taste, marinate the chicken breasts for 15 minutes before cooking in a mixture of olive oil, oregano, garlic powder, salt, and pepper. Add the chicken to the hot skillet and cook for 5-7 minutes per side or until golden brown and cooked through.
2. Transfer the chicken to a cutting board or platter. Sauté the diced onion in the pan for 3-4 minutes, stirring occasionally, until it softens and becomes translucent. Toss in the minced garlic and cook for one more minute, letting it become fragrant. Add the diced tomatoes with all their flavorful liquid. Bring to a simmer, then stir in the drained and rinsed cannellini beans. Reduce heat to low and simmer for 5 minutes until slightly thickening. Add the cooked chicken breasts back to the pan and spoon the sauce over them. Garnish with chopped fresh parsley, if desired. Serve this dish over a bed of cooked whole-wheat pasta or brown rice for a more complete meal. Or simply complement the dish with roasted veggies.

Crispy Chicken Gyros with Tzatziki Sauce

COOK: 30 MINS I SERVES: 2 I CAL: 400 KCAL PER SERVING

Ingredients

For the Chicken:
- 1 boneless, skinless chicken breast
- 1/4 cup plain Greek yogurt
- 1 tbsp lemon juice
- 1 tbsp olive oil
- 1 tsp dried oregano
- 1/2 tsp garlic powder
- 1/2 tsp dried thyme
- 1/4 tsp salt
- 1/4 tsp black pepper

For Serving:
- 2 small whole wheat pitas
- 1/4 cup crumbled red onion
- 1/4 cup chopped tomato *Lettuce (opt.)

For the Tzatziki Sauce:
- 1/2 cup plain Greek yogurt
- 1/4 cup grated cucumber (seeded if necessary)
- 1 tbsp olive oil
- 1 tbsp fresh dill, chopped (or 1 tsp dried dill)
- 1 clove garlic, minced
- Pinch of salt
- Pinch of black pepper

Instructions:

1. In a bowl, whisk together Greek yogurt, lemon juice, olive oil, oregano, garlic powder, thyme, salt, and pepper. Add chicken breast and toss to coat. Cover and refrigerate for at least 10 or 30 minutes for extra flavor.
2. Make the Tzatziki Sauce: In a separate bowl, combine Greek yogurt, grated cucumber (strain the grated cucumber over a bowl to remove excess moisture), olive oil, dill, garlic, salt, and pepper. Stir well and set aside. Heat a large skillet over medium heat. Add the chicken and cook for 5-7 minutes per side or until cooked through and golden brown. Remove from heat and let rest for 5 minutes. While the chicken rests, heat the pitas according to package instructions (usually in a microwave or toaster oven). Slice the chicken breast into thin strips. Spread some tzatziki sauce on each pita bread. Top with chicken, red onion, tomato, and lettuce (if using). Wrap it up and enjoy!

Spanish Beef & Bell Pepper Skillet

COOK: 25 MINS I SERVES: 2 I CAL: 450 KCAL PER SERVING

Ingredients

- 1 tbsp olive oil
- 1 medium onion, chopped (about 1 cup)
- 1 green bell pepper, chopped (about 1 cup)
- 1 pound ground beef (90% lean or lower)
- 1 tsp ground cumin

- 1/4 tsp garlic powder
- 1/4 tsp dried oregano
- 1 (14.5-ounce) can diced tomatoes, undrained
- 1/2 cup low-sodium beef broth
- 1/2 tsp smoked paprika

- 1/4 cup chopped fresh cilantro (optional)
- Chopped fresh parsley (optional) for garnish
- Salt and freshly ground black pepper to taste

Instructions:

1. Gather your ingredients and preheat a large skillet over medium heat. While the pan heats, chop the onion and bell pepper. Add the olive oil to the hot skillet. Once shimmering, add the diced onion and sauté in the pan for 3-4 minutes, stirring occasionally, until it softens and becomes translucent. Add the chopped bell pepper and saute for 2 minutes or until they've softened slightly.
2. Increase the heat to medium-high. Add the ground beef to the skillet and crumble it with a spoon as it cooks. Season with cumin, smoked paprika, garlic powder, and oregano. Cook the beef for 5 minutes, turning occasionally, until it's nicely browned and cooked. Drain any excess grease.
3. Next, pour in the canned diced tomatoes with all their juices, followed by the low-sodium beef broth. Stir to combine and bring to a simmer. Lower heat to medium-low and simmer 10 minutes, thickening slightly. Season with salt and pepper to taste. Remove the skillet from the heat. Stir in chopped fresh cilantro for an extra pop of flavor (optional). Garnish with chopped fresh parsley, if desired. Serve immediately over quinoa, cooked brown rice, or cauliflower rice.

Beef Kefta Kebabs with Mint Yogurt Sauce

COOK: 25 MINS I SERVES: 2 I CAL: 350 KCAL PER SERVING

Ingredients

For the Kebabs:
- 1 pound ground beef (90% lean or higher)
- 1/2 medium onion, finely grated
- 1/2 cup fresh parsley, chopped
- 2 cloves garlic, minced
- 1 tsp ground cumin

- 1/2 tsp dried oregano
- 1/2 tsp smoked paprika
- Salt and freshly ground black pepper, to taste
- 1 tbsp olive oil

For the Mint Yogurt Sauce:
- 1 cup plain Greek yogurt
- 1/4 cup chopped fresh mint
- 1 tbsp lemon juice
- 1 clove garlic, minced
- Salt and freshly ground black pepper, to taste

Instructions:

1. Make the Kebabs: In a large bowl, combine ground beef, grated onion, chopped parsley, minced garlic, cumin, oregano, paprika, salt, and pepper. Give your kebabs a kick with a sprinkle of cayenne pepper. Mix the ingredients with your hands until no streaks of dry ingredients remain. Don't overmix, be gentle!
2. Shape the Kebabs: Lightly wet your hands and form the mixture into 8-10 small kebabs.
3. Heat the Grill: Preheat your grill or grill pan to medium-high heat. Brush the kebabs with olive oil. Grill the kebabs for 5-7 minutes per side or until cooked through.
4. Make the Mint Yogurt Sauce: While the kebabs are cooking, whisk together lemon juice, Greek yogurt, minced garlic, chopped mint, salt, and pepper in a small bowl. Serve the hot kebabs with a dollop of mint yogurt sauce, and enjoy!

One-Pan Steak Fajitas with Peppers & Onions

COOK: 30 MINS I SERVES: 2 I CAL: 500 KCAL PER SERVING

Ingredients

- 1 pound flank steak, thinly sliced against the grain (Tip: Ask your butcher to slice it thin for fajitas)
- 1 tbsp olive oil
- 1 red bell pepper, thinly sliced
- 1 yellow bell pepper, thinly sliced
- 1 medium onion, thinly sliced

- 1 tbsp fajita seasoning (or substitute with a mixture of 1 tsp chili powder, 1/2 tsp ground cumin, 1/4 tsp smoked paprika, and a pinch of garlic powder)
- 1/2 lime, juiced (optional)
- Salt and freshly ground black pepper, to taste

Optional toppings (serve on the side):
- Warm tortillas (flour or corn)
- Shredded cheese (Monterey Jack, cheddar or a Mexican blend)
- Chopped avocado, Salsa
- Sour cream

Instructions:

1. In a large bowl, toss the sliced steak with olive oil, fajita seasoning, and a squeeze of lime juice (if using). Set aside to marinate for 10 minutes (while you prep the veggies). Marinate for more flavor: If you have extra time, marinate the steak for up to 30 minutes for an even deeper fajita flavor. Make fajitas with the classic flank steak, or try skirt steak or sirloin for a twist. To ensure maximum tenderness, grab a sharp knife and slice thinly against the muscle fibers. Meanwhile, preheat your oven to 400°F (200°C). Heat a large oven-safe skillet over medium-high heat. Add the peppers and onions to the pan. Sauté them for 5-7 minutes, until softened and slightly browned at the edges. Season with salt and pepper to taste. Push the vegetables to one side of the pan. Add the marinated steak to the empty side of the pan and sear for 2-3 minutes per side or until cooked to your desired doneness (rare, medium-rare, medium). Once cooked, stir the steak and vegetables together. Taste and adjust seasonings with additional salt, pepper, or lime juice. Add a pinch of cayenne pepper for a kick. Don't wait! Enjoy your sizzling fajitas immediately with warm tortillas and a fiesta of toppings!

Beef Kofta Meatballs with Marinara Sauce

COOK: 30 MINS I SERVES: 2 I CAL: 450 KCAL PER SERVING

Ingredients

For the Meatballs:
- 1 pound lean ground beef (90/10)
- 1/2 medium red onion, finely chopped
- 2 cloves garlic, minced
- 1/2 cup fresh parsley, chopped (divided use)
- 1 tbsp olive oil
- 1 tsp ground cumin

- 1/2 tsp dried oregano
- 1/2 tsp salt
- 1/2 tsp black pepper

For the Marinara Sauce:
- 1 (14.5-ounce) can crushed tomatoes
- 1/2 cup low-sodium chicken broth
- 1 tbsp tomato paste

- 1 tsp dried basil
- 1/2 tsp dried oregano
- Pinch of red pepper flakes (optional)
- Salt and freshly ground black pepper, to taste

Instructions:

1. In a large bowl, combine ground beef, onion, garlic, half of the parsley (reserve the other half for garnish), olive oil, cumin, oregano, salt, and pepper. Mix well using your hands until evenly combined. With wet hands, roll the meatball mixture into 12-16 evenly sized balls. Heat a large skillet over medium heat. Add the meatballs and cook for 5-7 minutes per side, or until browned on all sides. Make the Marinara: While the meatballs cook, combine crushed tomatoes, chicken broth, tomato paste, basil, oregano, and red pepper flakes (if using) in a saucepan. Season with salt and pepper to taste. Bring to a simmer. Once the meatballs are browned, carefully transfer the meatballs to the simmering marinara sauce. Turn the heat down to low, put on a lid, and let it simmer gently for 10-12 minutes. Check for doneness and a slightly thicker sauce. Remove from heat and garnish with remaining fresh parsley. Serve hot with your favorite sides.

Beef Bowls with Hummus & Feta

COOK: 30 MINS I SERVES: 2 I CAL: 500 KCAL PER SERVING

Ingredients

- 1 tbsp olive oil
- 1 pound ground beef (90% lean or higher recommended)
- 1/2 tsp dried oregano
- 1/4 tsp dried thyme
- 1/2 tsp garlic powder
- 1/4 tsp salt
- 1/4 tsp black pepper
- 1 cup cherry tomatoes, halved
- 1/2 cucumber, diced
- 1 cup cooked long-grain white rice (or brown rice for added fiber)
- 1/2 cup hummus (plain or your favorite flavor)
- 1/4 cup crumbled feta cheese
- 2 tbsps chopped fresh parsley

Instructions:

1. Wash and halve the cherry tomatoes. Dice the cucumber. Chop the fresh parsley if using.
2. In a large skillet, heat olive oil over medium heat. Add the ground beef and cook, breaking it up with a spoon until browned throughout, about 5-7 minutes. Drain any excess grease.
3. Stir in the oregano, thyme, garlic powder, salt, and pepper. For a spicy twist, toss in some red pepper flakes with the dried oregano and thyme. Cook for an additional minute, allowing the flavors to meld.
4. Divide the cooked rice evenly between two bowls. Top each bowl with half of the seasoned beef, cherry tomatoes, cucumber, hummus, feta cheese, and fresh parsley (if using).

Beef with Chickpeas and Apricots & plums

COOK: 30 MINS I SERVES: 2 I CAL: 450 KCAL PER SERVING

Ingredients

- 1 tbsp olive oil
- 1 pound boneless, skinless beef stew meat (cut into 1-inch cubes)
- 1/2 tsp salt
- 1/4 tsp black pepper
- 1 tsp ground cumin
- 1/2 tsp ground ginger
- 1/4 tsp turmeric
- 1/4 tsp cinnamon
- Pinch of cayenne pepper (adjust for desired spice level)
- 1 onion, chopped
- 2 cloves garlic, minced
- 1 (14.5-ounce) can diced tomatoes, undrained
- 1/2 cup low-sodium chicken broth
- 1 (15-ounce) can chickpeas, rinsed and drained
- 1/2 cup dried apricots, chopped
- 1/2 cup dried plums, chopped
- 1/4 cup chopped fresh cilantro

Optional Sides:
- Couscous
- Quinoa
- Steamed vegetables

Instructions:

1. In a small bowl, combine cumin, ginger, turmeric, cinnamon, and cayenne pepper. Wash and chop apricots and plums. Heat olive oil in a large skillet or Dutch oven over medium-high heat. Season beef with salt and pepper. This dish is even more flavorful if the beef is marinated in the spices for 30 minutes to an hour before cooking. Add beef and cook for 5-7 minutes, stirring occasionally, until browned on all sides. Stir in the spice mixture, onion, and garlic. Cook for 1 minute, until fragrant.
2. Pour diced tomatoes, chicken broth, chickpeas, apricots, and plums. Bring to a boil, then reduce heat to low, cover, and simmer 15-20 minutes, until beef shreds easily and sauce thickens. Remove from heat and garnish with fresh cilantro. Serve over couscous, quinoa, or steamed vegetables of your choice.

Greek Beef Burgers with Kefalograviera Cheese

COOK: 30 MINS I SERVES: 2 I CAL: 500 KCAL PER SERVING

Ingredients

- 1 pound ground beef (80/20 lean-to-fat ratio)
- 2 tbsps chopped fresh parsley
- 1 tbsp chopped fresh mint
- 1 tsp dried oregano
- 1/2 tsp garlic powder
- 1/4 tsp salt
- 1/4 tsp black pepper
- 1/4 cup finely chopped red onion
- 4 ounces crumbled kefalograviera cheese (or feta)
- 2 hamburger buns
- Olive oil for cooking

Optional toppings:
Sliced tomato, red onion, lettuce, crumbled cucumber, tzatziki sauce

Instructions:

1. In a large bowl, combine ground beef, red onion, parsley, mint, oregano, garlic powder, salt, and pepper. Mix gently until just combined.
2. Divide the mixture into two equal portions and form them into slightly larger patties than your hamburger buns. Preheat your grill pan or skillet over medium heat. Add a drizzle of olive oil.
3. Gently place the burger patties in the pan and cook for 5-7 minutes per side or until desired doneness.
4. In the last minute of cooking, crumble half of the kefalograviera cheese (kefalograviera cheese can sometimes be hard to find, you can use feta cheese instead) over each burger patty. Let the cheese melt slightly.
5. Place the cooked burgers on toasted hamburger buns (if using). For extra flavor, toast your hamburger buns in a skillet with olive oil while the burgers cook. Add your favorite toppings and enjoy!

Steak & Chimichurri Sauce with Sweet Potatoes

COOK: 30 MINS I SERVES: 2 I CAL: 500-600 KCAL PER SERVING

Ingredients

For the Steak:
- 2 boneless ribeye steaks (each about 6 oz / 170 g)
- 1 tbsp olive oil
- Salt and freshly ground black pepper, to taste

For the Roasted Sweet Potatoes:
- 1 medium sweet potato, peeled and cut into 1-inch cubes (about 2 cups)
- 1 tbsp olive oil
- 1/2 tsp dried oregano, 1/4 tsp garlic powder
- 1/4 tsp smoked paprika (optional)
- Salt and freshly ground black pepper

For the Chimichurri Sauce:
- 1/2 cup fresh flat-leaf parsley, chopped
- 1/4 cup fresh cilantro, chopped (optional)
- 2 cloves garlic, minced
- 1 tbsp red wine vinegar
- 1/4 cup olive oil
- 1/4 tsp red pepper flakes (opt.)
- Salt and freshly ground black pepper, to taste

Instructions:

1. Preheat oven to 425°F (220°C). In a medium bowl, toss sweet potato cubes with olive oil, oregano, garlic powder, paprika (if using), salt, and pepper. Arrange the potatoes in an even layer on the baking sheet. Pat steaks dry with paper towels. Season generously with salt and pepper. Heat a large skillet over medium-high heat. Add olive oil and swirl to coat. Sear steaks for 3-4 minutes per side for medium-rare or to your desired doneness. Transfer steaks to a plate and tent with foil to let them rest for 5 minutes. While the steaks are resting, bake the sweet potatoes for 15-20 minutes or until tender and golden brown, tossing halfway through. Chimichurri: In a small bowl, combine parsley, cilantro (if using), olive oil, garlic, red wine vinegar, red pepper flakes (if using), salt, and pepper. Stir well. Slice steak thinly against the grain. Arrange steak slices on plates with roasted sweet potatoes. Spoon chimichurri sauce over the steak and potatoes. Enjoy!

One-Pan Meat Shakshuka Rice Bowl

COOK: 25 MINS I SERVES: 2 I CAL: 450 KCAL PER SERVING

Ingredients

- 1 tbsp olive oil
- 1/2 onion, diced
- 1 clove of garlic, minced
- 1 pound ground beef (or ground lamb, sausage, or turkey)
- 1/2 tsp smoked paprika
- 1 (14.5-ounce) can diced tomatoes, undrained
- 1/2 cup low-sodium chicken broth
- 1/4 cup chopped fresh parsley
- 1 tsp ground cumin
- 1/2 cup cooked white rice (basmati or jasmine recommended)
- 2 large eggs
- Salt and freshly ground black pepper, to taste
- 1/4 cup crumbled feta cheese

Instructions:

1. Heat olive oil in a large skillet over medium heat. While the oil heats, dice the onion and mince the garlic. Chop the parsley leaves and crumble the feta cheese. Prepare the rice as directed on the packaging. Sauté the diced onion in the hot skillet for 3-4 minutes or until tender. Add the minced aromatic garlic and cook it for another minute, stirring frequently. Add the ground meat to the pan and crumble it with a spoon as it cooks. Season with smoked paprika, cumin, salt, and pepper. Cook for 5-7 minutes until the meat is browned . Pour the vibrant diced tomatoes, including flavorful juices, and chicken broth into the pan. Stir well, loosening any delicious browned bits stuck to the bottom. Bring the mixture to a simmer and cook for 5 minutes, allowing the flavors to meld. Stir in the cooked white rice and chopped parsley. Taste and adjust salt and pepper as desired.
2. Using a spoon, create two shallow wells in the simmering tomato mixture. Carefully crack an egg into each well. Cover the skillet and turn the heat down to low. Cook the eggs until the whites are solidified and the yolks reach your preferred level of doneness, about 5-7 minutes. Take the pan off the heat source and crumble the feta cheese over the top. Serve immediately with crusty bread for dipping.

Lemon Garlic Pork Chops

COOK: 30 MINS I SERVES: 2 I CAL: 350 KCAL PER SERVING

Ingredients

- 2 tbsps extra virgin olive oil
- 2 cloves garlic, thinly sliced
- 1 lemon, thinly sliced
- 2 bone-in, center-cut pork chops (about 6-8 ounces each)
- 1/2 tsp dried oregano
- 2 fresh bay leaves
- 1/2 tsp salt
- 1/4 tsp freshly ground black pepper

Optional Sides (not included in calorie count):
- Roasted vegetables (broccoli, asparagus, zucchini)
- Steamed rice or quinoa

Instructions:

1. In a small dish, combine the oregano, salt, and pepper. Heat olive oil in a large skillet over medium-high heat. Add the garlic and bay leaves. Cook, stirring occasionally, until the garlic becomes fragrant, about 30 seconds. Season the pork chops with the oregano mixture. Carefully add the pork chops to the pan and sear for 3-4 minutes per side, or until golden brown. Add the lemon slices to the pan and squeeze the juice from half the lemon over the pork chops. Turn down the heat to medium-low. Cook for 3-4 minutes, or until the juices run clear when you pierce the thickest part of the pork chops with a knife. Transfer the pork chops to plates and spoon the pan drippings with the garlic and lemon over them. Garnish with the remaining lemon slices (optional) and serve immediately with your chosen sides.

DESSERTS & DRINKS

Greek Yogurt with Honey & Nuts

COOK: 15 MINS | SERVES: 2 | CAL: 280 KCAL PER SERVING

Ingredients

- 1 cup plain Greek yogurt (2% or whole milk fat)
- 1/4 cup chopped walnuts
- 2 tbsps honey
- 1/2 tsp ground cinnamon (optional)

Instructions:

1. Grab two bowls and spoon that yummy yogurt in – equal portions for everyone!
2. Sprinkle half the chopped nuts on each yogurt mountain. Roasted nuts? YES PLEASE! Toast those walnuts in a pan for a few minutes for a deeper flavor (watch them closely so they don't burn!).
3. Drizzle with honey to your heart's content (or until your taste buds dance happily).
4. Feeling fancy? Dust with a pinch of cinnamon for some extra flavor fun. Fruit lover? Fresh berries or chopped dried fruit are delicious additions.

Vanilla Lemon Summer Mousse

COOK: 20 MINS | SERVES: 6 HALVES | CAL: 200 KCAL (1 H.)

Ingredients

- 100 ml of lemon juice (freshly squeezed for that sunshine punch!)
- 1 tsp of vanilla extract
- 10 g of gelatin
- 150 ml of whipping cream
- 50 g of sugar (add more if you have a sweet tooth, less if you like it tart)
- Mint leaves (optional)

Instructions:

1. Grab your lemon and halve it! Scrape out all that lovely zest, then squeeze out all the juice you can. Put the juice in a saucepan with the sugar and gelatin. Stir it all together until it's smooth.
2. In another bowl, whip that cream until it forms stiff peaks.
3. Now, slowly whisk the lemon mixture into the whipped cream. Be gentle, like folding a cloud!
4. Grab a sieve (like a strainer) and pour the whole mixture through it. This catches any lumps and makes your mousse super smooth. Time to chill! Pour the mousse into serving glasses (or lemon halves like in the picture) and pop them in the fridge for at least 1 hour. To enhance the aroma, add a sprig of mint for a touch of summer freshness before serving.

Whipped Ricotta with Berries

COOK: 15 MINS I SERVES: 2 I CAL: 200 KCAL PER SERVING

Ingredients

- 1/2 cup whole-milk ricotta cheese
- 2 tbsps powdered sugar (for a richer flavor, substitute 1 tbsp of the powdered sugar with honey)
- 1/2 tsp vanilla extract
- Fresh mint leaves for garnish (optional)
- 1/4 cup fresh mixed berries (strawberries, blueberries, raspberries)

Instructions:

1. In a medium bowl, using a hand mixer or a whisk, beat the ricotta cheese, powdered sugar, and vanilla extract until smooth and creamy, about 2-3 minutes. Want to make it vegan? Use a vegan ricotta cheese alternative and maple syrup instead of honey.
2. Divide the whipped ricotta mixture between two serving bowls.
3. Gently arrange the fresh berries in each bowl on top of the ricotta.
4. Garnish with a sprig of fresh mint, if desired. Serve immediately.
Tip: Add a squeeze of fresh lemon juice to the whipped ricotta for a touch of tartness.

Baked Apples with Cinnamon & Walnuts

COOK: 30 MINS I SERVES: 4 I CAL: 250 KCAL PER SERVING

Ingredients

- 4 large apples (such as Granny Smith, Honeycrisp, or Gala)
- 1/4 cup chopped walnuts
- 2 tbsps unsalted butter, melted
- 2 tbsps brown sugar, packed
- 1/4 tsp ground nutmeg (optional)
- 1/4 cup water
- 1 tsp ground cinnamon

Instructions:

1. Preheat oven to 375°F (190°C). Lightly grease a baking dish.
2. Wash and core the apples. Take out the cores of the apples using either a sharp knife or an apple corer. Leave the bottom intact.
3. In a small bowl, combine melted butter, brown sugar, cinnamon, and nutmeg (if using). Stir until well combined.
4. Stuff the apple cavities with the walnut mixture. If there's extra filling, sprinkle it around the apples in the baking dish. Add water to the preheated oven's bottom baking dish to prevent burning.
5. Bake for 15-20 minutes, or until the apples soften and yield to the touch, and the filling simmers and bubbles merrily. Baste the apples with the pan juices halfway through baking for extra flavor. Let cool slightly before serving.

Fruit Salad with Mint & Pistachios

COOK: 10 MINS I SERVES: 2 I CAL: 200 KCAL PER SERVING

Ingredients

- 1 kiwi, peeled and sliced
- 1 apple, cored and chopped
- 1 orange, peeled and segmented (cut into supreme segments by slicing off the peel and membrane, then separating the flesh)
- 1/2 cup strawberries, hulled and halved (or quartered)
- 1/2 cup blueberries
- 2 tbsps chopped fresh mint
- 2 tbsps chopped pistachios
- Juice of 1/2 lemon (optional)

Instructions:

1. Wash and prepare all fruits. Peel and slice the kiwi, core, and chop the apple (to prevent browning, toss the apples in a little lemon juice after chopping), segment the orange, and hull and halve (or quarter) the strawberries. In a medium bowl, combine the kiwi, apple, orange, strawberries, and blueberries.
2. Gently toss in the chopped mint and pistachios.
3. Add half a lemon juice for a touch of extra tang. However, this is optional!

Serving Suggestions:

4. Enjoy this fruit salad chilled for an extra refreshing treat.
5. Drizzle with a touch of honey or maple syrup for additional sweetness (not included in calorie count).
6. Serve alongside yogurt or a scoop of vanilla ice cream for a complete dessert.

Sesame Seed Halva with Honey

COOK: 20 MINS I SERVES: 6 I CAL: 350 KCAL PER SERVING

Ingredients

- 1/2 cup raw honey
- 1/2 cup tahini (sesame seed paste)
- 1/4 cup chopped toasted pistachios (optional)
- Pinch of sea salt
- 1 tsp vanilla extract (optional)

Instructions:

1. Heat the honey over low heat in a small saucepan until it simmers and becomes bubbly. Be careful not to overheat or burn the honey. Combine with Tahini: Remove the honey from heat and pour it into a medium bowl. Whisk in the tahini until well combined. The mixture will thicken considerably. If using, fold in the chopped pistachios and a pinch of sea salt. For a silky texture, heat the honey, then pulse it with the tahini in a food processor. Want to experiment with flavors? Mix 1 teaspoon of vanilla extract or a pinch of ground cinnamon into the honey-tahini mixture.
2. Cool and set: Gently ladle (or spoon) the rich halva mixture into a low-sided baking dish prepared with a parchment paper sling. Smooth the top with a spoon. Let the halva cool completely at room temperature, or for a faster set, place it in the refrigerator for 15 minutes. Serve and Enjoy! Cut the halva into squares, and enjoy! Store leftover halva in an airtight container in the fridge for up to a week.

Dates Stuffed with Almonds & Orange Zest

COOK: 10 MINS I SERVES: 2 I CAL: 200 KCAL PER SERVING

Ingredients

- 10 Medjool dates (pitted)
- 10 whole almonds
- 1 orange (zested)

Instructions:

1. Prep the dates: Wash and dry the Medjool dates. With a controlled hand and a sharp blade, create a precise incision along the side of each date, forming a small pocket.
2. Stuff and zest: Gently press an almond into the pocket of each date. Using a fine-holed grater or zester, zest the orange over the stuffed dates, coating them evenly. For a richer flavor, give the almonds a dry roast in a skillet over medium heat for 2-3 minutes, until they turn golden brown. Let them cool slightly before stuffing the dates.
3. Want a chocolate twist? Dip the stuffed dates in melted dark chocolate (cocoa content 70% or higher for a healthy option) and refrigerate for 15 minutes to set.

Yogurt Bark with Berries & Granola

COOK: 10 MINS I SERVES: 2 I CAL: 200 KCAL PER SERVING

Ingredients

- 1 cup (150g) plain Greek yogurt (2% or non-fat)
- 1/4 cup (35g) mixed berries (fresh or frozen)
- 1/4 cup (30g) granola (your favorite kind, preferably with nuts and seeds)
- 1 tbsp (15ml) honey (optional)

Instructions:

1. Fit a sheet of parchment paper into your small baking sheet, making sure it covers the base. Smooth the yogurt into an even layer on the baking sheet, creating a layer about ¼ inch thick. Gently press the berries into the yogurt. You can arrange them in a pattern for a more decorative look, or simply scatter them evenly.
2. Sprinkle the granola over the yogurt and berries. If desired, drizzle the honey over the top for a touch of sweetness. Feel free to experiment with different types of berries, such as blueberries, raspberries, strawberries, or blackberries. If you don't have granola, you can substitute chopped nuts or seeds.
3. For optimal results, freeze the baking sheet for a minimum of 2 hours or until the yogurt is completely frozen solid.
4. When ready to serve, break the yogurt bark into pieces and enjoy!

Baked Figs with Goat Cheese & Honey

COOK: 20 MINS I SERVES: 2 I CAL: 220 KCAL PER SERVING

Ingredients

- 4 fresh figs (ripe but firm)
- 2 oz soft goat cheese
- 1 tbsp Honey
- Fresh thyme (optional, for garnish)

Instructions:

1. Preheat your oven to 400°F (200°C). Line a baking sheet with parchment paper.
2. Wash and dry the figs. Cut a small "X" into the top of each fig, without cutting all the way through.
3. Using a spoon, gently open the figs and fill each cavity with a dollop of goat cheese.
4. Place the stuffed figs on the prepared baking sheet. Drizzle each fig with a touch of honey. For a more complex taste, ditch the honey and drizzle with balsamic glaze.
5. Bake for 10-12 minutes, or until the figs are softened and slightly caramelized.
6. Take the dish out of the oven and allow it to cool for a few minutes before serving. For an extra touch, garnish with a sprinkle of fresh thyme leaves. Don't have fresh thyme? A pinch of dried thyme or a sprinkle of chopped fresh rosemary will work too.

Honey-Roasted Pears with Walnuts

COOK: 25 MINS I SERVES: 2 I CAL: 250 KCAL PER SERVING

Ingredients

- 4 ripe pears (Bosc, Anjou, or Concorde are goodchoices)
- 4 tablespoons honey
- 1/2 tsp ground cinnamon
- Pinch of ground nutmeg (optional)
- 1/4 cup chopped walnuts, toasted

Instructions:

1. Preheat your oven to 400°F (200°C). Lightly grease a baking sheet. Wash and dry the pears. Cut them in half lengthwise and core them using a spoon or melon baller. In a small bowl, whisk together the honey, cinnamon, and nutmeg (if using).
2. Place the pear halves cut-side up on the prepared baking sheet. Brush each pear generously with the honey mixture. For a richer flavor, add a tablespoon of unsalted butter to the honey mixture before brushing it on the pears. Sprinkle the toasted walnuts evenly over the pears. If you don't have toasted walnuts, you can toast them in a dry skillet over medium heat for a few minutes, watching them closely to avoid burning. Roast for 20-25 minutes, or until the pears are tender when pierced with a fork but not mushy. The juices should be bubbling slightly around the edges. Let the pears cool slightly before serving. Enjoy them warm or at room temperature.

Citrus Symphony Salad

COOK: 20 MINS I SERVES: 2 I CAL: 250 KCAL PER SERVING

Ingredients

For the Citrus Syrup:
- 1 large lemon (zest only)
- 2 tbsp honey
- 1/4 cup water
- 1 vanilla bean (seeds scraped)
- Fresh basil or mint (optional)

The Citrus Ensemble:
- 1 orange (sliced), 1 blood orange (sliced or segmented)
- 1 grapefruit (segmented)
- 1 kiwi (sliced)
- 1/2 pink grapefruit (segmented)
- Pomegranate seeds (for garnish)

Instructions:

1. Syrup Simmer: Grab your lemon and a veggie peeler. Get just the yellow zest, leaving the white pith behind. Throw the zest in a small pot with honey, water, vanilla bean seeds (or extract), and 1 tablespoon of lemon juice. Heat it up on medium for 5-8 minutes, stirring sometimes, until it thickens a bit and smells amazing. Take it off the heat and toss the lemon peel (and vanilla pod if you used one).
2. Fruit Fiesta: Slice your oranges into rounds. For the grapefruit, follow the same method, but instead of rounds, cut it into segments by following the membranes. Slice your kiwi and toss all this fruity goodness aside.
3. The Big Mix: Grab a bowl and toss in all your sliced citrus and kiwi. Drizzle with the cooled citrus syrup and give it a gentle mix to coat everything. Are you feeling fancy? Add some chopped basil or mint for an extra layer of freshness (totally optional!). Serve the salad straight from the bowl for a casual vibe. Throw in some pomegranate seeds for a pop of color and sweetness. This citrus salad is a flavor and texture explosion, so grab your favorite people (or your couch!), and enjoy this vitamin C powerhouse!

Chocolate Avocado Mousse

COOK: 10 MINS I SERVES: 2 I CAL: 300 KCAL PER SERVING

Ingredients

- 1 ripe avocado, halved and pitted
- 3 tbsps unsweetened cocoa powder
- 2 tbsps maple syrup or honey
- 1 tbsp milk of choice (dairy or non-dairy)
- 1/2 tsp vanilla extract
- Pinch of sea salt

Instructions:

1. Dig out the avocado flesh and toss it in a blender. Super ripe avocados are essential for the best texture.
2. Throw in the cocoa powder, maple syrup, milk, vanilla, and salt. Dark chocolate cocoa powder makes it extra rich (yum!). If it's too thick, add a little more milk by the tablespoon until it's perfect.
3. Blend it all up until it's smooth and creamy, scraping the sides if needed.
4. Split the mousse between 2 bowls.
5. (Optional) Fancy it up with a sprinkle of cocoa powder, some whipped cream, or fresh berries (if you have them on hand).

Greek Yogurt Panna Cotta

COOK: 20 MINS I SERVES: 2 I CAL: 250 KCAL PER SERVING

Ingredients

- 1 tbsp unflavored gelatin
- 2 tbsps cold water
- 1 cup whole milk plain Greek yogurt (strained for extra thickness, optional)
- 1/2 cup low-fat milk
- 1/4 cup granulated sugar
- 1/2 tsp vanilla extract
- Fresh berries (optional, for garnish)

Instructions:

1. In a small bowl, gently scatter the gelatin powder over the cold water. Let the mixture sit undisturbed for 5 minutes, allowing the gelatin to absorb the water and become softened.
2. In a small saucepan, combine the low-fat milk and sugar. Gently heat the mixture over medium heat, watching until the sugar crystals vanish completely and the mixture simmers gently. Do not boil. Remove the milk mixture from heat and whisk in the softened gelatin until fully dissolved. Let it cool slightly for a few minutes.
3. In a medium bowl, give the Greek yogurt and vanilla extract a good whisking. Slowly whisk in the cooled milk mixture until well combined. Strain the Greek yogurt for a thicker and smoother panna cotta. For a richer flavor, use full-fat Greek yogurt. Divide the panna cotta mixture between two ramekins or small glasses. Cover with plastic wrap and refrigerate for at least 4 hours, or until set. Get creative with toppings! Chopped nuts, a drizzle of citrus syrup, or a sprinkle of cocoa powder are all delicious options. Let the vibrant berries take center stage when serving (optional) and enjoy your cool and creamy Greek yogurt panna cotta!

Fig & Almond Bars

COOK: 25 MINS I SERVES: 2 I CAL: 280 KCAL PER SERVING

Ingredients

- 1/2 cup dried figs, chopped
- 1/2 cup rolled oats
- 1/4 cup sliced almonds
- 1 tbsp honey
- 1 tbsp (15ml) olive oil
- 1/4 tsp ground cinnamon
- Pinch of salt

Instructions:

1. Preheat your oven to 180°C (around 350°F). Grab a baking sheet and line it with some parchment paper.
2. In a bowl, toss together the chopped figs, oats, almonds, honey, olive oil, cinnamon, and salt. Make sure everything gets nice and coated. Want more chew? Throw in a tablespoon of chopped dried cranberries. Feeling fancy? Swap the honey for a drizzle of maple syrup.
3. Press the mixture firmly onto the baking sheet, spreading it evenly. Think of it like making a yummy, healthy pizza crust.
4. Bake for 15-20 minutes or until it has a beautiful, golden brown finish and smells amazing. Patience is key here – let them cool completely on the baking sheet before cutting into bars (we know it's tempting!).

Mini Filo Nut Pies

COOK: 30 MINS I SERVES: 2 I CAL: 150 KCAL PER FILO

Ingredients

- 1/4 cup chopped walnuts (or pecans, pistachios - you pick!)
- 1/4 cup chopped almonds
- 2 tbsps chopped dried figs (apricots work too!)
- 1 tbsp honey (maple syrup or agave nectar in a pinch)
- 1 tbsp olive oil
- 1 tsp ground cinnamon
- 1/4 teaspoon ground nutmeg
- Pinch of salt
- 5 sheets of filo pastry (thawed as per package directions)
- Melted butter (around 3 tbsps - go light on the butter brush!)

Instructions:

1. Crank your oven to 375°F (190°C) and grab a mini muffin tin (10 cups should do). Lightly grease those wells for happy little filo cups! In a bowl, toss your chopped nuts, dried fruit, honey, olive oil, spices, and salt. Play around with the nuts and dried fruits! Explore different options to find your perfect combo.
2. Grab a sheet of filo pastry and lay it flat. Brush it with some melted butter (light hand!). Don't drown the filo in butter! A light brushstroke is all you need for crispy perfection. Drape another sheet on top and give it another butter brush. Repeat this with three sheets total, making a yummy buttered stack. Cut your filo stack into 10 squares. Gently press each square into a greased mini muffin cup, forming a little well for the filling. Divide your nut mixture evenly among the 10 filo cups. Pop those cups in the oven for 10-12 minutes or until the filo is a deep, rich gold and shatteringly crisp. - that's your cue! Let the cups cool slightly before digging in. You can enjoy them warm or at room temperature - it is totally up to you! Nom Nom!

Greek Yogurt Banana Bread

COOK: 25 MINS I SERVES: 2 I CAL: 350 KCAL PER SERVING

Ingredients

- 1 cup (think about a generous handful) all-purpose flour
- 1/2 tsp baking soda
- 1/4 tsp salt (a pinch will do)
- 1/4 cup plain Greek yogurt (whole milk or 2% for extra creaminess)
- 1 super ripe banana, mashed (the riper, the better!)
- 1/4 cup maple syrup (honey or agave nectar work too, if you're out)
- 1 egg
- 2 tbsps melted butter
- 1/2 tsp vanilla extract (optional, but adds a nice touch)
- 1/4 cup chopped walnuts or pecans

Instructions:

1. Preheat your oven to 350°F (175°C). Grab a small loaf pan (about 4x8 inches) or two mini loaf pans and grease them. Whisk together the flour, baking soda, and salt in a bowl. Set it aside for a second.
2. In another bowl, mash your banana like there's no tomorrow. Super ripe bananas = super moist bread. The browner, the better! Stir in the Greek yogurt, melted butter, maple syrup, egg, and vanilla extract (if using) until everything's happy and combined. Slowly add the dry ingredients to the wet ones, mixing until combined. Don't overdo it! If you're using nuts, fold them in gently. Are you feeling fancy? Gently fold in 1/4 cup of chocolate chips or chopped dried fruit with the nuts. Pour the batter into your greased pan(s). Bake for about 20 minutes. The bake time can vary slightly, so keep an eye on it. You'll know it's done when a toothpick inserted in the center comes out clean. Give it 5 minutes in the pan, then transfer to a wire rack to finish cooling.

Chia Seed Pudding with Fruit & Nuts

COOK: 10 MINS I SERVES: 2 I CAL: 250 KCAL PER SERVING

Ingredients

- 1/2 cup plant-based milk (think almond, cashew, whatever you like!)
- 1/4 cup plain Greek yogurt (optional for extra creaminess)
- 1/4 cup chia seeds
- 1 tbsp honey or maple syrup (or more if you have a sweet tooth)
- Pinch of cinnamon
- Fresh fruit (berries, banana slices, mango – go wild!)
- 1/2 tsp vanilla extract
- 1/4 cup chopped nuts and/or seeds (almonds, walnuts, pumpkin seeds)

Instructions:

1. Grab a jar or container with a lid. Toss in the milk, yogurt (if using), chia seeds, honey, vanilla, and cinnamon. Want a thicker pudding? Use less milk (¾ cup milk to 1/2 cup chia seeds).
2. Give it a good stir to break up any clumps. Seal it tight and shove it in the fridge for at least 4 hours or overnight for a thicker pudding.
3. When you're ready to dig in, spoon the chia pudding into bowls and top with your favorite fruits and nuts - the more colorful, the better!

Matcha Chia Pudding

COOK: 10 MINS I SERVES: 2 I CAL: 230 KCAL PER SERVING

Ingredients

- 1 cup plant-based milk (almond milk is a good choice, but use your fave!)
- 1/3 cup chia seeds
- 1 tsp matcha powder
- 1 tbsp maple syrup (or honey)
- 1/2 tsp vanilla extract
- Fresh mint leaves and sliced almonds (for garnish)

Instructions:

1. Grab a bowl or jar and whisk together your plant-based milk, chia seeds, matcha powder, maple syrup, and vanilla extract. Like a boss! Want it super creamy? Use full-fat coconut milk instead of almond milk. Is matcha a little too strong? Just use less powder! Is your sweet tooth acting up? Add more maple syrup or honey to taste.
2. Stick a lid on that container and shove it in the fridge for at least 4 hours, or better yet, overnight. The chia seeds have to soak up all that goodness and get nice and thick.
3. When you're ready to chow down, spoon that pudding into two bowls.
4. Top it off with sliced almonds or some granola for an extra fancy (but easy) touch. Feeling fruity? Layer in your favorite chopped fruits like strawberries, blueberries, or mango.

Fig & Walnut Blast Smoothie

COOK: 15 MINS | SERVES: 2 | CAL: 300 KCAL PER SERVING

Ingredients

- 1 cup of your fave plant-based milk (think almond, cashew, oat – you pick!)
- 1/2 cup frozen pitted dates (or 4-5 dates, if you're feeling fancy)
- 1/4 cup chopped walnuts
- 1/2 frozen banana
- 1/2 tsp ground cinnamon
- 1/4 tsp vanilla extract
- Pinch of sea salt
- Ice cubes (optional, for a thicker smoothie)
- 2 chopped dried figs (fresh work too)

Instructions:

1. Throw everything in your blender and hit blend! Aim for smooth and creamy, scraping down the sides if needed. Fresh figs? Awesome! Adjust the amount based on how sweet you like things. Start with 1 and add more for a sweeter smoothie. Are dates a little hard? Soak them in hot water for 10 minutes for a creamier blend.This recipe is naturally vegan and gluten-free – high five! Want it sweeter? Add more dates or a drizzle of honey/maple syrup. Are you feeling adventurous? This is your base! For an added energy punch, mix in some protein powder, a handful of spinach for a green boost, or chia seeds for extra fiber. Are ice cubes needed for a thicker smoothie? Add them now!
2. Taste test and adjust sweetness or spices as you see fit.
3. Pour into glasses and enjoy that deliciousness!

Spiced Yogurt Smoothie

COOK: 10 MINS | SERVES: 2 | CAL: 250 KCAL PER SERVING

Ingredients

- 1 cup (240ml) plain Greek yogurt (go for the good stuff!)
- 1/2 cup (120ml) frozen fruit (mango, berries, mix it up!)
- 1/2 cup (120ml) unsweetened almond milk (or your fave plant-based milk)
- 1/4 teaspoon ground ginger
- 1/4 teaspoon ground cinnamon
- Pinch of cayenne pepper
- (optional, for a spicy kick)
- Ice cubes (optional, if you like it frosty)

Instructions:

1. Throw everything in a blender. Frozen fruit makes it thicker and colder (perfect for those hot days!). No frozen fruit? No worries! For a chilly treat, add some ice cubes and toss in fresh fruit. Spice it up (or not)! For a subtle kick, begin with a pinch of cayenne and add more for a fire in your mouth (in a good way). Want it creamier? Use whole milk yogurt. Are you feeling fancy? Boost the protein content by adding some protein powder, nut butter, or spinach for an extra boost. Blend it up smooth like a boss.
2. Taste and adjust if needed – sweeter? Spicier? You're the master!
3. Pour, sip, and enjoy your delicious and nutritious creation!

Sparkling Water with Berries & Mint

COOK: 5 MINS I SERVES: 2 I CAL: 30 KCAL PER SERVING

Ingredients

- 1 cup fresh berries (any kind you like – strawberries, blueberries, raspberries, go wild!)
- 1/4 cup mint leaves (fresh is best, but a few slices of cucumber or lemon work in a pinch)
- 2 cups chilled sparkling water (grab your favorite brand!)
- Ice cubes (optional, for an extra frosty blast)

Instructions:

1. Rinse those berries (gotta keep things clean!). Muddle a few mint leaves in a glass (basically smash them gently to release their excellent flavor). No mint? No worries! Cucumber or lemon slices provide a touch of invigorating freshness.
2. Toss in the berries and ice (if using). Craving a hint of sweetness? Muddle a few berries with the mint for some natural flavor. Honey or agave nectar work too (use a light hand, though). Make it fancy! Throw in a sprig of mint and a few berries for garnish – instant Instagram-worthy drink!
3. Top it all off with that chilled sparkling water.
4. Give it a quick stir, and BAM! You've got a delicious drink.

Avocado Spinach Mango Smoothie

COOK: 10 MINS I SERVES: 2 I CAL: 250 KCAL PER SERVING

Ingredients

- 1/2 avocado, nice and ripe (pit and peel that bad boy)
- 1 cup frozen mango chunks (fresh works too, but add some ice cubes)
- 1 cup spinach, gotta get those greens in! (Fresh or frozen)
- 1/2 cup unsweetened almond milk (any plant-based milk you like works!)
- Squeeze of lime juice (about 1/2 a lime)
- 1/4 teaspoon ground cinnamon (optional, but adds a nice touch)

Instructions:

1. Throw everything in your blender and blend it well until it's smooth and creamy. Scrape down the sides if needed. Want it thicker? Use less milk or add a spoonful of chia seeds or flaxseed meal. No fresh spinach? No problem! Use 1/2 cup frozen instead. Is your sweet tooth acting up? Drizzle with honey or maple syrup. This smoothie is your blank canvas! Feeling fancy? Throw in a scoop of protein powder for an extra punch. Do you have berries on hand? Toss some in for a burst of antioxidants.
2. Too thick? Add a splash more milk, one tablespoon at a time, until it's just right.
3. Pour into glasses and enjoy that deliciousness!

Pumpkin Spice Smoothie

COOK: 10 MINS I SERVES: 2 I CAL: 250 KCAL PER SERVING

Ingredients

- 1 frozen banana (chopped into chunks)
- 1/2 cup canned pumpkin puree (not pie filling!)
- 1/2 cup plain Greek yogurt (frozen yogurt works too)
- 1/2 cup milk of your choice (almond milk is a winner, but use what you've got!)
- 1 tbsp maple syrup (or honey, if you're feeling it)
- 1/2 tsp cinnamon
- 1/4 tsp nutmeg
- Pinch of ginger (optional)

Instructions:

1. Add all the ingredients to your blender and whirl them together on high until the mixture is completely smooth and has a luxuriously creamy texture. No pumpkin pie spice? No worries! Just mix 1/2 teaspoon each of cinnamon, nutmeg, and ginger. Want to pump up the protein? For a protein boost, add one scoop of your preferred protein powder. Are you feeling fancy? Drizzle some maple syrup or honey on top before you sip. Need a thickness boost? Add a cup of tender baby spinach or chopped kale. They'll blend right in!
2. Sip and adjust the sweetness or spices to your liking.
3. Pour into glasses and enjoy!

Tropical Sunshine Smoothie

COOK: 10 MINS I SERVES: 2 I CAL: 200 KCAL PER SERVING

Ingredients

- 1 cup frozen mango chunks (in cubed form!)
- 1/2 cup frozen pineapple chunks
- 1 frozen banana (ripe for extra sweetness, but not mushy)
- 3/4 cup plant-based milk (almond, coconut)
- 1 tbsp lime juice (fresh is best, but bottled works in a pinch)

Add-Ins (optional, but fun):

- 1/4 cup plain Greek yogurt (adds a protein punch)
- 1/4 tsp ground ginger
- Handful of baby spinach (nobody will even notice the green!)

Instructions:

1. Throw everything in a blender. Is your blender not the strongest? If you want a better consistency, thaw the frozen fruit for a short while before blending. Like it sweeter? Use a riper banana. Want it thinner? Add more milk. Thicker? Less milk! Feeling fancy? Add the yogurt for a creamier smoothie. Not a fan of mango? Swap it for papaya, peaches, or berries!
2. Blend it up well until it's smooth and dreamy.
3. Pour it into a glass and enjoy that tropical taste!

Watermelon Mint Cooler Smoothie

COOK: 10 MINS | SERVES: 2 | CAL: 250 KCAL PER SERVING

Ingredients

- 4 cups cubed watermelon (think half a small watermelon, chopped up)
- 1 tbsp mint leaves (plus a little extra for garnish)
- 1/4 cup plain yogurt (go for non-dairy if that's your thing)
- 1/4 cup water (add more if you want it thinner, no sweat!)
- 1 tbsp honey (optional, if your watermelon isn't sweet enough)
- Pinch of sea salt (optional, for an extra pop)

Instructions:

1. Wash and chop that watermelon into cubes. Seeds? Toss those out! Freeze your watermelon chunks overnight for an extra frosty treat.
2. Wash and chop up your mint leaves. Don't love mint? Swap it for some basil leaves!
3. Throw everything in a blender and blend it smooth like a boss. Take a sip! Is it too sweet? Not sweet enough? Add honey or water to your taste. Want it thinner? Add more water, a splash of lime juice, or even coconut water.
4. Pour it into glasses and add a sprig of mint on top for some extra pizzazz (optional).
5. Gulp it down and enjoy that excellent, refreshing taste!

Homemade Refreshing Ginger Ale

COOK: 25 MINS | SERVES: 2 | CAL: 50 KCAL PER SERVING

Ingredients

- 2 cups water
- 1 inch knob of ginger (think thumb-sized), peeled and sliced thin
- 1/3 cup honey (or agave nectar, maple syrup for vegans)
- Juice from 1/2 a lemon
- Club soda, nice and chilled (as much as you like for fizz)
- Lime wedges for garnish (optional, but pretty!)

Instructions:

1. Boil the water in a pot, then toss in the ginger slices. Let it simmer for 5 minutes, like a ginger spa for your kitchen. Take it off the heat and let it steep for another 10 minutes, letting all that good flavor mingle. Tip: Want it extra gingery? Simmer for an additional 5 minutes. Like it hotter? Use more ginger or leave the peel on while simmering.
2. Grab a strainer and pour the ginger tea into a bowl, leaving the ginger bits behind. Now, add your honey (or your favorite sweetener) and stir it in until it's all dissolved. Let it cool down a bit – you don't want it scalding hot!
3. Fizz Time! Fill two glasses with ice. Are you feeling adventurous? Try flavored sparkling water instead of club soda – grapefruit, lemon-lime, or even ginger flavored water, would be delicious! Pour the cooled ginger tea into each glass, then top it off with club soda until it's as bubbly as you like. Want more tang? Squeeze in some fresh lemon juice. Garnish with a lime wedge for some extra flair (totally optional, but fun!).

CONCLUSION

You nailed it! You've officially become a Mediterranean master chef (or at least a really awesome home cook). Your kitchen probably smells fantastic right now, and hopefully, your taste buds are doing a happy dance. Remember, this isn't some rigid diet – it's a flavor fiesta! Don't be afraid to mix things up. Swap ingredients based on what's fresh, get creative with spices and make these recipes your own. The Mediterranean is all about flexibility and fresh flavors.

Honestly, you might find yourself feeling like a superhero after a while – more energy, better mood, the whole shebang. That's because this isn't just about the food; it's about an entire way of life. It's about slowing down, enjoying the company, and appreciating the simple pleasure of a delicious meal. So next time you cook, crank up some music, grab some friends, and savor the moment (not the dirty dishes – we'll deal with those later!). This book is just the beginning. Keep exploring, keep experimenting, and keep that olive oil flowing! You've got this!

I'd love to hear your thoughts! Leave a review on Amazon and help others discover this book.

ENJOY EXCLUSIVE BONUS RECIPE VIDEOS! SIMPLY SCAN THE QR CODE, ENTER YOUR EMAIL, AND WE'LL SEND YOU A LINK TO ACCESS THESE DELICIOUS TREATS.

"

THE MEDITERRANEAN DIET ISN'T JUST ABOUT WHAT YOU EAT, IT'S ABOUT SLOWING DOWN AND SAVORING THE MOMENT. SAVOR THE FOOD, SAVOR THE COMPANY, SAVOR LIFE.

- LEONORA GROVER

YOUR MEAL PLAN: WEEK 1

	BREAKFAST	LUNCH	DINNER
MEATLESS MONDAY	Creamy Ricotta Toast with Honey & Berries (blueberry) p.16	Greek Salad p.38	Feta Garlic Pasta with Vegetables (make extra veggies for the next day) p.57
TUNA TUESDAY	Whipped Feta with Roasted Vegetables Toast p.18	Tuna Salad with White Beans & Artichokes p.40	Lemon Garlic Chicken with Roasted Vegetables p.72
WEDNESDAY	Greek Yogurt Power Bowl with Berries (or any other fruits) & Granola p.22	Lemon Garlic Chicken with Roasted Vegetables p.72	Vegetarian Moussaka (make extra portions for the next day) p.61
TASTY THURSDAY	Spiced Chickpea Scramble with Feta & Herbs p.20 (use leftover feta from Lentil Salad)	Leftover Vegetarian Moussaka p.60	Baked Cod with Puttanesca Sauce p.66
FANCY FRIDAY	Strawberry Balsamic Oats p.23	Quinoa Nuts Salad with Roasted Veggies (use leftover veggies from Baked Cod with Puttanesca Sauce) p.40	Crispy Falafel Bowls with Tahini Sauce (make extra portions for next day) p.59
SAVORY SATURDAY	Scrambled Eggs, Kalamata Olives & Tomatoes p.24	Leftover Crispy Falafel Bowls with Tahini Sauce p.59	One-Pan Spiced Chickpea Buddha Bowl (make extra portions for next day) p.61
SUPER SUNDAY	Honey-Almond Ricotta Pancakes with Berries p.27	Leftover One-Pan Spiced Chickpea Buddha Bowl p.61	Dinner buffet featuring leftover dishes throughout the week

YOUR MEAL PLAN: WEEK 2

	BREAKFAST	LUNCH	DINNER
MEATLESS MONDAY	Scrambled Eggs with Feta & Tomatoes Toast p.17	Quinoa Mango Salad with Honey-Lime Vinaigrette p.44	Greek Baked Beans in Tomato Sauce, Greek Island Cabbage Salad p.60,44
TROPICAL TUESDAY	Tropical Sunshine Oats with Mango & Chia Seeds (plan to cook on Monday evening) p.21	Leftover Greek Baked Beans in Tomato Sauce p.60	Pan-Seared Salmon, Lemon, Herbs, Green Asparagus, Tomatoes & Parmesan p.63, 34
WEDNESDAY	Whipped Feta with Roasted Vegetables Toast p.18	Leftover Pan-Seared Salmon, Lemon, Herbs, Green Asparagus, Tomatoes & Parmesan p.63, 34	Caramelized Onion Pasta p.60
TASTY THURSDAY	Creamy Fig & Walnut Overnight Oats (plan to cook on Wednesday evening) p.22	Leftover Caramelized Onion Pasta p.60	Honey Dijon Chicken with Goat Cheese, Crispy Garlic Brussels Sprouts p.73, p. 37
FANCY FRIDAY	Sun-Kissed Scramble Wrap p.15	Leftover Honey Dijon Chicken with Goat Cheese p.73	Veggie Quinoa Power Bowl Soup p.51
SAVORY SATURDAY	Sweet Potato Pancakes with Maple Syrup & Pecans p.27	Sun-Kissed Salad with Burrata & Figs p.43	Eggplants & Creamy Garlic Buratta Tomatoes p.58
SUPER SUNDAY	Poached Egg & Salmon Toast with Avocado p.19	Leftover Veggie Quinoa Power Bowl Soup p.51	Greek Beef Burgers, Tzatziki, Greek Roasted Beet Salad & Goat Cheese p.80, 38

YOUR MEAL PLAN: WEEK 3

	BREAKFAST	LUNCH	DINNER
MEATLESS MONDAY	Greek Yogurt Power Bowl with Berries (or any other fruits) & Granola p.22	Summer Quinoa Salad with Feta & Mint p.41	Sunshine Pasta with Zesty Herb Sauce p.58
TOMATO TUESDAY	Sun-Dried Tomato & Goat Cheese Toast with Arugula p.17	Arugula Protein Salad with Veggies & Feta p.43	Greek-Style Baked Cod with Potatoes & Tomatoes p.67
WEDNESDAY	Almond & Orange Blossom Chia Pudding (plan to cook on Tuesday evening) p.21	Leftover Greek-Style Baked Cod with Potatoes & Tomatoes p.67	Stuffed Bell Peppers with Feta, Mushrooms & Herbs p.62
TUSCAN THURSDAY	Smoked Salmon & Avocado Delight Wrap p.15	Leftover Stuffed Bell Peppers with Feta, Mushrooms & Herbs p.62	Skillet Chicken with Sun-Dried Tomatoes & Spinach p.75
FANCY FRIDAY	Creamy Ricotta Toast with Honey & Berries (blueberry, strawberries, raspberries) p.16	Leftover Skillet Chicken with Sun-Dried Tomatoes & Spinach p.75	Moroccan Carrot Chickpea Stew with Lemon p.49
SAVORY SATURDAY	Italian Sausage & Scrambled Eggs with Spinach p.25	Leftover Moroccan Carrot Chickpea Stew with Lemon p.49	Zucchini Fritters, Tzatziki Greek Salad p.29
SUPER SUNDAY	Honey-Almond Ricotta Pancakes with Berries p. 27	Classic Greek Salad p.38	Green Asparagus Risotto with Shrimp p.64

YOUR MEAL PLAN: WEEK 4

	BREAKFAST	LUNCH	DINNER
MEATLESS MONDAY	Creamy Fig & Walnut Overnight Oats (cook on Sunday evening) p.22	Leftover Green Asparagus Risotto with Shrimp p.64	Warm Couscous Veggie Salad p.45
TASTY TUESDAY	Scrambled Eggs with Feta & Tomatoes Toast p.17	Leftover Warm Couscous Veggie Salad p.45	Citrusy Red Cabbage Salad with Cheese & Nuts, Pan-Seared Salmon p.45, 63
WEDNESDAY	Tropical Sunshine Oats with Mango & Chia Seeds (plan to cook on Tuesday evening) p.21	Leftover Citrusy Red Cabbage Salad with Cheese & Nuts, Pan-Seared Salmon p.45, 63	Creamy Tomato & Tortellini Soup p.50
TUSCAN THURSDAY	Spicy Black Bean & Avocado Toast, Lime Crema p.19	Leftover Creamy Tomato & Tortellini Soup p.50	Tuscan Chicken with White Beans p.76
FANCY FRIDAY	Scrambled Eggs, Kalamata Olives & Tomatoes p.24	Leftover Tuscan Chicken with White Beans p.76	Orzo with Roasted Veggies p.62
SAVORY SATURDAY	Strawberry Balsamic Oats p.23	Leftover Orzo with Roasted Veggies p.62	Arugula Protein Salad with Veggies & Feta p.43
SUPER SUNDAY	Caprese Frittata with Fresh Basil p.25	Spiced Chickpea Fritters & Lemon Yogurt Sauce p.33	Steak & Chimichurri Sauce with Sweet Potatoes p.80

Made in the USA
Las Vegas, NV
27 November 2024

12247702R00057